P
Pl

Masnoon Du'âin

Translated by
M. Abdul Hameed Siddiqui

Islamic Book Service (P) Ltd.
New Delhi

PRAYERS OF THE PROPHET ﷺ
(Masnoon Duaaen)

Translated by
M. Abdul Hameed Siddiqui

ISBN 978-81-7231-219-0

First Published 2000
Nineteenth Impression 2019

Published by *Abdus Sami* for :

Islamic Book Service (P) Ltd.

1516-18, Pataudi House, Darya Ganj, New Delhi-2 (India)
Tel.: +91-11-23244556, 23253514, 23269050, 23286551
e-mail: info@ibsbookstore.com
Website: www.ibsbookstore.com
amazon.in www.bit.do/ibs

WORLDWIDE DISTRIBUTORS

U.K	–	Azhar Academy Limited, London
U.S.A	–	Al Minar Book & Islamic Fashion, Philadelphia
India	–	Husami Book Depot, Hyderabad
Ghana	–	Marhaba Book Shop, Accra
Canada	–	NHK Impex, Ontario
Pakistan	–	Paramount Books, Karachi
Maldives	–	Fahiya Enterprises, Male
Indonesia	–	Lautan Lestari (Lestari Books), Jakarta
Sri Lanka	–	Islamic Book House, Colombo
Singapore	–	Tranquil Hearts Gifts
South Africa	–	Sawant's Creations, Cape Town

Printed in India

PREFACE

This is a translation of the prayers of the Holy Prophet (ﷺ) entitled Masnoon Duaain called from the Pages of the Holy Qur'an and authentIc works of Traditions. The Prophet Was a great believer in Prayers: supplications his Lord With a Zeal and fervour rarely to be found the reIigious literature of the world. One who cares to read them, cannot but be overwhelmed with the depth of feelings with which he addressed Allah, intense love of the Great Master, deep consciousness of His unbounded favours, unshakable confidence in the Divine Mercy, and unfaltering faith in his Might and Power and sense of deep humility-these are the multicoloured threads with which is woven the delicate pattern of the Prophet's (ﷺ) prayers.

In this age of gross materialism, a book dealing with prayers may have no great charm. The modern man is so much absorbed in the material pursuits that he may not find time to respond effectively to the yearnings of his soul. But in the midst of this turmoil he sometimes finds himself in the grip of a terrible void and his soul sets out itself frantically in search of spiritual peace. It is on this occasion that ne finds solace and comfort in prayers.

Prayer is the life .and soul of man's existence. It is the natural urge of man which is inseparably essential for him. I believe that the need for prayers has never been so pressing and great as today when man, under the impact of the materialism, has been forced to live as a soulless human being bereft of all tender feelings to which he owes his superiority to all the created things.

Publisher

CONTENTS

Special Prayer for Everyone

بِسْمِ اللَّهِ الرَّحْمَنِ الرَّحِيمِ

اَللَّهُ لَا اِلهَ اِلَّا هُوَالْحَيُّ الْقَيُّومُ O الٓمٓ O اَللَّهُ لَآ اِلهَ

اِلَّا هُوَ الْحَيُّ الْقَيُّومُ O وَعَنَتِ الْوُجُوهُ لِلْحَيِّ

الْقَيُّومِ لَا اِلهَ اِلَّا اَنْتَ سُبْحَانَكَ اِنِّى كُنْتُ مِنَ

الظَّالِمِينَ يَا اَحَدُ الصَّمَدُ O الَّذِى لَمْ يَلِدْ O وَلَمْ

يُوْلَدْ O وَلَمْ يَكُنْ لَّهُ كُفُوًا اَحَدُ (يَا اَرْحَمَ الرَّحِمِينَ

O ظَلَمْنَا اَنْفُسَنَا وَاِنْ لَّمْ تَغْفِرْ لَنَا وَتَرْحَمْنَا

لَنَكُوْنَنَّ مِنَ الْخَسِرِينَ O رَبَّنَا اغْفِرْلَنَا وَتُبْ عَلَيْنَا

اِنَّكَ اَنْتَ التَّوَّابُ الرَّحِيْمُ O رَبِّ اغْفِرْ وَارْحَمْ

وَتَجَاوَزْ عَنْ مَّا تَعْلَمُ اِنَّكَ اَنْتَ الْاَعَزُّ الْاَكْرَمُ اَللَّهُمَّ

اِنَّكَ عَفُوٌّ كَرِيْمٌ تُحِبُّ الْعَفْوَ فَاعْفُ عَنَّا اَللَّهُمَّ

مُصَرِّفَ الْقُلُوْبِ صَرِّفْ قُلُوْبَنَا عَلَى طَاعَتِكَ

يَامُقَلِّبَ الْقُلُوْبِ ثَبِّتْ قُلُوْبَنَا عَلَى دِيْنِكَ اَللَّهُمَّ اِنَّ

قُلُوبَنَا وَنَوَاصِيَنَا وَجَوَارِحَنَا بِيَدِكَ لَمْ تُمَلِّكْنَا
مِنْهَا شَيْئًا فَاِذَا فَعَلْتَ ذَالِكَ بِنَا فَكُنْ اَنْتَ وَلِيَّنَا
وَاهْدِنَا اِلٰى سَوَآءِ السَّبِيلِ اَللّٰهُمَّ اَرِنَا الْحَقَّ حَقَّا
وَّارْزُقْنَا اِتِّبَاعَهُ وَاَرِنَا الْبَاطِلَ بَاطِلًا وَّارْزُقْنَا
اِجْتِنَابَهُ اَللّٰهُمَّ ارْزُقْنَا حُبَّكَ وَحُبَّ رَسُوْلِكَ وَحُبَّ
مَنْ يَّنْفَعُنَا حُبُّهُ عِنْدَكَ يَا حَيُّ يَا قَيُّوْمُ بِرَحْمَتِكَ
نَسْتَغِيْثُ نَسْتَغْفِرُكَ رَبَّنَا وَنَسْئَلُكَ التَّوْبَةَ وَاَصْلِحْ
لَنَا شَاْنَنَا كُلَّهُ وَلَا تَكِلْنَا اِلٰى اَنْفُسِنَا طَرْفَةَ عَيْنٍ
فَاِنَّكَ اِنْ تَكِلْنَا اِلٰى ضُعْفٍ وَّ عَوْرَةٍ وَّ ذَنْبٍ وَّ خَطِيْئَةٍ
اَللّٰهُمَّ لَا سَهْلًا اِلَّا مَا جَعَلْتَهُ سَهْلًا وَاَنْتَ تَجْعَلُ
الْحُزْنَ سَهْلًا اِذَا شِئْتَ لَآ اِلٰهَ اِلَّا الْحَلِيْمُ الْكَرِيْمُ
سُبْحَانَ اللّٰهِ رَبِّ الْعَرْشِ الْعَظِيْمِ اَلْحَمْدُ لِلّٰهِ رَبِّ
الْعَالَمِيْنَ نَسْئَلُكَ مُوْجِبَاتِ رَحْمَتِكَ وَعَزَآئِمَ
مَغْفِرَتِكَ وَالْغَنِيْمَةَ مِنْ كُلِّ بِرٍّ وَّالسَّلَامَةَ مِنْ كُلِّ اِثْمٍ

لَا تَدَعْ لَنَا ذَنْبًا اِلَّا غَفَرْتَهُ يَآ اَرْحَمَ الرَّاحِمِيْنَ وَلَا

هَمًّا اِلَّا فَرَّجْتَهُ وَلَا حَاجَةً هِىَ لَكَ رِضًا اِلَّا

قَضَيْتَهَا يَآ اَرْحَمَ الرَّاحِمِيْنَ اِلَيْكَ رَبِّ فَحَبِّبْنَا وَفِىْ

اَنْفُسِنَا لَكَ رَبِّ فَذَلِّلْنَا وَفِىْ اَعْيُنِ النَّاسِ فَعَظِّمْنَا

وَمِنْ سَيِّئِ الْاَخْلَاقِ فَجَنِّبْنَا وَعَلٰى صَالِحِ

الْاَخْلَاقِ فَقَوِّمْنَا وَعَلٰى صِرَاطِ الْمُسْتَقِيْمِ فَثَبِّتْنَا

وَعَلَى الْاَعْدَآءِ اَعَدَّ آئِكَ اَعْدَآءِ الْاِسْلَامِ فَانْصُرْنَا

اَللّٰهُمَّ انْصُرْنَا وَلَا تَنْصُرْ عَلَيْنَا اَللّٰهُمَّ امْكُرْلَنَا وَلَا

تَمْكُرْ عَلَيْنَا اللّٰهُمَّ زِدْنَا وَلَا تَنْقُصْنَا وَلَا

تُسَلِّطْ عَلَيْنَا مَنْ لَّايَرْحَمُنَا اللّٰهُمَّ اشْرَحْ صُدُوْرَنَا

لِلْاِسْلَامِ اللّٰهُمَّ حَبِّبْ اِلَيْنَا الْاِيْمَانَ وَزَيِّنْهُ فِىْ

قُلُوْبِنَا وَكَرِّهْ اِلَيْنَا الْكُفْرَ وَالْفُسُوْقَ وَالْعِصْيَانَ

سُبْحَانَ رَبِّكَ رَبِّ الْعِزَّةِ عَمَّا يَصِفُوْنَ وَسَلِّمْ عَلٰى

الْمُرْسَلِينَ وَالْحَمْدُ لِلّهِ رَبِّ الْعَلَمِينَ ِ اٰمِين يَا رَبَّ
الْعَلَمِينَ O

Bismillâhir-Rahmânir-Rahîm

Allâhu la ilâha illa huwal hayyul qayyumu alif-lâm-mîm. Allâhu lâ ilâha illa huwal hayyul qayyum. Wa anatil wujûho lil hayyil qayyûṃ. Lâ ilâha illa anta subhanaka inni kuntu minaz-zâlimîn. Yâ ahadas-samadal-lazi lam yalid wa lam yulad. Wa lam yakul-lahu kufuwan ahad. Yâ arhamar-râhimîn zalamana anfusana. Wa illam taghfirlana wa tarhamna la nakûnanna minal-khasirîn. Rabbanaghfir-lana wa tuba-laina in-naka antat-tawwab-ur-rahîm rabbighfir warham wa tajawaz-am-ma ta-lam innaka antal a-azzul-akram. Allâhumma innaka afuwwun karîmun tuhibbul afwa fa'fu 'anna. Allâhumma musarrifal-qulûb sarrif qulûbana 'ala ta'atika ya muqallibal-qulûb Thabbit qulûbana 'ala dînika Allâhumma inna qulûbana wa nawasiena wá jawarihna beyadika lam tumallikna minha shai-an fa-iza fa-alta zalika bina fakun anta waliyana wahdina ila sawa-is-sabîl.

Allâhumma arinal haqqa haqqan warzuqna ittiba ahu wa arinal batila batilan warzuqna ijtinabahu allahum-mar–zuqna hubbaka wa hubba rasûlika wa hubba many-yanfau-na hubbuhu indaka ya hayyu ya qayyûmu bi-rahmatika nastaghîsu nastagh-firuka rabbana wa nasalukat-taubata wa aslih lana shanana kullahu wala takilna ila anfusina tarfata 'ainin fa-innaka in tukilna ila dhofinw wa auratinw wa zambinw Wa khatieatin. Allâhumma la sahla illa ma ja'altahu sahlan wa anta tajalul huzna sahlan iza shita. Lâ ilaha illal-halîmul-karimu subhanal-lahi rabbil arshil-azîm. Al-hamdu-lillâhi rabbil-âlamîn nas-aluka-mujibâti-rahmatika wa aza-ima maghfiratika walghanimata min kulli birrin was-salâmata min kulli ismin la tad'u lana zamban illa

ghafartahu ya arhamar-rahimîn wala
hamman illa far-rajtahu wala hâjatan hiya
laka rizan illa qazaitaha ya arhamar râhimîn
ilaika rabbi fahabbibna wa fi anfusina laka
rabbi fazal-lilna wa fi a'ayuninnasi fa
azzimna wa min sayyi-il akhlaqi fajannibna
wa ala salihil-akhlaqi faqawwimna wa ala-
siratil-musta-qîmi fasabbitna wa alal âdai-i-
adâika ada-il islami fansurna Allâhum-
mansurna wala tansur alaina. Allâhum-
mamkurlana wala tamkur alaina.
Allâhumma zidna wala tanqusna wala tu-
sallit alaina malla yarha-muna Allâhum-
mashrah-sudûrana lil Islami. Allâhumma
habbib ilainal-imana wa zayyinhu fî
qulûbina wakarrih ilainal-kufra wal-fusuqa
wal isyana Subhana Rabbika rabbil-izzati
'amma yasifûn wa salamun alal mursalîn
wal hamdu lillâhi Rabbil âlamin. Âmîn ya
Rabbal âlamîn.

In the Name of Allâh, The Most Gracious, The Most Merciful

Allâh! There is no god but He, the Ever-Living, the Self-Subsisting, by Whom all subsist. Alif-Lâm-Mîm-Allâh! There is no god but He, the Ever-Living, the Self-subsisting, by Whom all subsist. And downcast will be the faces before the Living, the Self-Subsisting. There is no god but Thee; Thy Glory I extol. Verily, I have been of the wrongdoers. O One Absolute and Independent! He who begets not nor is He begotten. And none bears likeness to Him. O Most Merciful of the mercifuls! We have wronged ourselves, And if Thou forgivest us not, And bestowest not upon us Thy Mercy. We shall certainly be of the losers. Our Lord! Forgive us, and turn to us (mercifully); surely Thou art the Oft-Returning (to Mercy), the

Merciful. O Lord! Forgive, and take mercy and overlook, what Thou knowest (about our deeds); Thou art the Most Respectful and Most Gracious. O Allâh! Thou art Most Forgiving and Kind. Thou lovest forgiveness. Kindly forgive us, O Allâh! Turner of the hearts, turn our hearts to Thy obedience. O Director of hearts! Keep our hearts steadfast to Thy religion, O Allâh! Verily our hearts, our forelocks and our limbs are in Thy hand. Thou hast not given us control over any one of them. When Thou hast ordained so in our case, Thou (alone) be our Protector, and guide us to the even way. O Allâh! Show us the Truth as Truth, and render us help to follow that; and show us falsehood as falsehood, and help us to avoid that. O Allâh! Endow us with Thy love and the love of Thy Messenger, and the love of that which is beneficent for us in Thy eyes. O Ever-Living and Self-

-Subsisting! Unto Thy Mercy we appeal and ask forgiveness. O our Lord! We ask repentance; set right all our affairs; and entrust us not, even for the twinkling of an eye, to ourselves for if Thou entrustest us to ourselves, Thou in fact entrustest us to weakness and faultiness, sin and offence. O Allâh! Nothing is easy; save that which Thou makest it so, and Thou makest the difficult easy whensoever Thou likest. There is no God besides Him, the Forbearing, the Magnanimous. Pure is He, the Master of the Highest Throne. Praise is for Him only, the Lord of all the worlds; we ask of Thee the qualities which move. Thy Grace and Forgiveness; and the opportunity of doing every kind of good and protection against every kind of sin. Let no sin of ours remain unforgiven, O Merciful of the mercifuls! No worry unremoved; and no want; which is according to Thine liking, unsatisfied O Merciful of the mercifuls! O Lord! Endow us Thy love and instill in our hearts; a yearning for submission to Thee, and exalt us in the eyes of the people, and protect us against adopting a wrong behaviour, and (give us strength) to stand firmly on the right conduct and to the straight path, and against (our) enemies, Thy enemies, the enemies of Islam.

Help us, O Allâh! Help us, and we beseech Thee not to lend (anyone) and help against us. O Allâh! Order our affairs for us, and do not manipulate affairs against us. O Allâh! Make us prosperous, and decrease us not, and impose not upon us a ruler, who takes no pity upon us. O Allâh! Open our hearts for Islam. O Allâh! Make faith something cherished for us, and embellish with that our hearts; and make repulsive and hateful for us unbelief, immorality and transgression. O Allâh! Make us of those, who are rightly guided. Glory to the Lord, the Lord of Honour and Power (He is free) from what they ascribe (to Him) and Peace on the Messengers and Praise to Allâh the Lord and Cherisher of the Worlds.

PRAYERS FOR THIS WORLD AND THE HEREAFTER

اَللّٰهُمَّ اغْفِرْلِىْ وَارْحَمْنِىْ وَعَافِنِىْ وَارْزُقْنِىْ

Allâhummaghfirli warhamni wa âfini warzuqni

O Allâh! Forgive me, take pity upon me, preserve me, and grant me sustenance.

3

اَللّٰهُمَّ اَحْسِنْ عَاقِبَتَنَا فِى الْاُمُوْرِ كُلِّهَا وَ اَجِرْنَا مِنْ خِزْىِ الدُّنْيَا وَعَذَابِ الْاٰخِرَةِ

Allâhumma ahsin aqibatana fil umûri kulliha wa ajirna min khizyid-dunya wa azâbil âkhirati.

O Allâh! Make sublime in their outcome; all our actions; and save us from disgrace in this world, and from the chastisement in the Hereafter.

4

اَللّٰهُمَّ اَصْلِحْ لِیْ دِیْنِی الَّذِیْ هُوَ عِصْمَةُ اَمْرِیْ
وَاَصْلِحْ لِیْ دُنْیَایَ الَّتِیْ فِیْهَا مَعَاشِیْ وَ اَصْلِحْ لِیْ
اٰخِرَةَ الَّتِیْ فِیْهَا مَعَادِیْ وَاجْعَلِ الْحَیَاةَ زِیَادَةً لِّیْ
فِیْ کُلِّ خَیْرٍوَّاجْعَلِ الْمَوْتَ رَاحَةً لِیْ مِنْ کُلِّ شَرٍّ

*Allâhumma-aslih lî dîni-al-lazi huwa
ismatu amri wa asleh lî dunyayallati fiha
ma'ashi wa aslih lî âkhiratallati fiha ma'adi
waj alil hayata ziyadatal-lî fi kulli khairin waj
alil mauta râhatal-lî min kulli sharrin.*

O Allâh! Improve my religious life;
for that is to be my refuge; and improve
my worldly life, for I have to lie it; and
prepare me for the afterlife, to which I
shall have to return; and make this life a
mean to achieve every kind of good; and
turn death into a bliss before any evil
state, supervenes.

5

اَللّٰهُمَّ اِنِّىْ اَسْئَلُكَ الْعَفْوَ وَالْعَافِيَةَ فِى الدُّنْيَا

وَالْاٰخِرَةِ

Allâhumma inni asalukal afwa wal âfiyata fid-dunya wal âkhirati.

O Allâh! I beseech Thee for forgiveness and for protection in this world and the world Hereafter.

6

رَبِّ اغْفِرْلِىْ وَتُبْ عَلَىَّ اِنَّكَ اَنْتَ التَّوَّابُ الرَّحِيْمُ

اَللّٰهُمَّ اِنِّىْ ظَلَمْتُ نَفْسِىْ ظُلْمًا كَثِيْرًا وَّلَا يَغْفِرُ

الذُّنُوْبَ اِلَّا اَنْتَ فَاغْفِرْلِىْ مَغْفِرَةً مِّنْ عِنْدِكَ

وَارْحَمْنِىْ اِنَّكَ اَنْتَ الْغَفُوْرُ الرَّحِيْمُ

Rabbighfirli wa tub alayya innaka antat tawwabur-rahîm. Allâhumma inni zalamtu nafsî zulman kasîranw wala yaghfiruz-

zunûba illa anta faghfirli maghfiratam min indika war hamni innaka antal ghafûrur-rahîm.

O Allâh! Forgive me and turn to me; Thou art Most Forgiving and Merciful. O Allâh! I did a grave wrong to myself and none except Thee forgivest the sins. So grant me forgiveness from Thyself, and take pity upon me. Thou art the Most Forgiving. Most Merciful.

7

اَللّٰهُمَّ اقْسِمْ لَنَا مِنْ خَشْيَتِكَ مَاتَحُوْلُ بِهِ بَيْنَنَا

وَبَيْنَ مَعَاصِيْكَ وَمِنْ طَاعَتِكَ مَاتُبَلِّغُنَا بِهِ جَنَّتَكَ

وَمِنَ الْيَقِيْنِ مَاتُهَوِّنُ بِهِ عَلَيْنَا مَصَآئِبَ الدُّنْيَا

Allâhummaqsim-lana min khashya-tika ma tahûlu bihi bainana wa baiña ma'asika wa min ta-atika ma tuballighuna bihi jannataka wa minal yaqîni ma tohawwenu bihi alaina masâ-i-bad dunya.

O Allâh! Give us a part of Thy fear which may serve us as a barrier between us and the sins, and a part of yearning for "Thy obedience which may entitle us to Thy heaven, and a faith which may make easy for us the hardship of this world.

8

اَللّٰهُمَّ اَعِنِّيْ عَلٰى ذِكْرِكَ وَشُكْرِكَ وَحُسْنِ عِبَادَتِكَ

Allâhumma-a-inni ala zikrika wa shukrika wa husni ibadatika.

O Lord! Help me in remembering Thee, in expressing gratitude to Thee, and in worshipping Thee in the best of manners.

9

اَللّٰهُمَّ اِنَّكَ عَفُوٌّ تُحِبُّ الْعَفْوَ فَاعْفُ عَنِّيْ

Allâhumma innaka afuwwun tuhibbul afwa fa-fu anni.

O Allâh! Thou art the Most Forgiving, Thou lovest forgiveness, so forgive me.

10

اَللّٰهُمَّ اجْعَلْنِى صَغِيرًا فِى عَيْنِى وَكَبِيرًا فِى اَعْيُنِ النَّاسِ.

Allâhummaj alni Saghîran fî aini wa kabiran fî âyunin-nasi.

O Allâh! Make me insignificant in my own eyes and significant in the eyes of others.

11

اَللّٰهُمَّ طَهِّرْقَلْبِى مِنَ النِّفَاقِ وَعَمَلِى مِنَ الرِّيَاءِ وَلِسَانِىْ مِنَ الْكِذْبِ وَعَيْنِىْ مِنَ الْخِيَانَةِ فَاِنَّكَ تَعْلَمُ خَائِنَةَ الْاَعْيُنِ وَمَا تُخْفِى الصُّدُوْرُ.

Allâhumma tah-hir qalbi minan nifaqi wa amali minar-riya-i wa lisani minal kizbi wa aini minal khiyanati fa innaka tâlamu kha-i natal âyuni wa ma tukhfis-sudûro.

O Allâh! Purge my heart from hypocricy. My conduct from dissimulation, my tongue from falsehood and my eyes from treachery, for Thou indeed knowest the treacherous glance of the eyes and that which bosoms conceal.

12

اَللّٰهُمَّ اِنِّىْ اَعُوْذُ بِكَ مِنْ عِلْمٍ لَّا يَنْفَعُ وَقَلْبٍ لَّا يَخْشَعُ وَدُعَآءٍ لَّا يُسْمَعُ وَنَفْسٍ لَّا تَشْبَعُ

Allâhumma inni a'ûzubika min ilmil la yanfao wa qalbil la yakhshao wa du'â-il la yusmao wa nafsil la tashba-o

O Allâh! I seek 'Thy refuge from the knowledge that brings no good, and from the heart that has no fear (of Allâh), and from the prayer that cannot be entertained, and the self that cannot be satisfied.

13

رَبَّنَا لَا تُزِغْ قُلُوْبَنَا بَعْدَ اِذْهَدَ يْتَنَا وَهَبْ لَنَا مِنْ

لَّدُنْكَ رَحْمَةً اِنَّكَ اَنْتَ الْوَهَّابُ ه

Rabbana la tuzigh qulûbana bada is hadaitana wa hablana milladunka rahmatan innaka antal wahhab.

Our Lord, make not our hearts to deviate after Thou hast guide us, and grant us mercy; surely Thou art the Most Liberal Giver.

14

رَبِّ اجْعَلْنِيْ مُقِيْمَ الصَّلوٰةِ وَمِنْ ذُرِّيَّتِيْ رَبَّنَا

وَتَقَبَّلْ دُعَآءِ ه

Rabbij alni muqîmas-salâti wa min zurriyati rabbana wataqabbal du'â

My Lord, make me keep up prayer and also my offspring, O, Our Lord! And accept my prayer.

PRAYERS IN THE MORNING AND EVENING.

15

For Morning

أَصْبَحْنَا وَأَصْبَحَ الْمُلْكُ لِلّٰهِ رَبِّ الْعَٰلَمِيْنَ

As bahna wa asbahal mulku lil-lâhi rabbil âlamîn.

We enter upon morning and so doth the creation of Allâh, Lord of the worlds.

16

اَللّٰهُمَّ اِنِّيْ اَسْئَلُكَ خَيْرَ هٰذَا الْيَوْمِ فَتْحَهُ وَنَصْرَهُ وَنُوْرَهُ وَبَرَكَتَهُ وَهُدَاهُ وَاَعُوْذُ بِكَ مِنْ شَرِّ مَافِيْهِ وَ شَرِّمَا بَعْدَهُ

Allâhumma inni asaluka khaira hâzal yaumi fat-hahu wa nusrahu wa nûrahu wa barkatahu wa hudahu wa aûzubika min sharri ma fîhi wa sharri ma bâdahu.

O Allâh! I beg of Thee, the good of this day, the victory thereof, the help thereof, the light thereof, the blessing thereof; and the guidance thereof; and I seek refuge in Thee from the evil that be therein. And the evil that be thereafter.

17

اَللّٰهُمَّ اِنِّىۡ اَسۡئَلُكَ عِلۡمًا نَّافِعًا وَّرِزۡقًا وَّاسِعًا وَّعَمَلًا مُّتَقَبَّلًا وَّ شِفَاءً مِّنۡ كُلِّ دَآءٍ ؕ

Allâhumma inni asaluka ilman nafi-an wa rizqan wasi an wa amalam mutaqabbilan wa shifa-am min kulli dâyin

O Allâh! I beg of Thee useful knowledge, and abounding sustenance and commendable conduct and cure from all ailments.

18

For Dusk

اَمۡسَيۡنَا وَاَمۡسَى الۡمُلۡكُ لِلّٰهِ رَبِّ الۡعٰلَمِيۡنَ ؕ

Am-saina wa amsal mulku lil lâhi rabbil âlamîn.

We enter upon the evening, and so doth the creation of Allâh, Lord of the Worlds.

19

اَللّٰهُمَّ اِنّیْ اَسْئَلُكَ خَیْرَ هٰذِهِ اللَّیْلَةِ فَتْحَهَا وَ نَصْرَهَا

وَنُوْرَهَا وَبَرَكَتَهَا وَهُدَاهَا وَاَعُوْذُ بِكَ مِنْ شَرِّ مَا

فِیْهَا وَشَرِّ مَا بَعْدَهَا.

Allâhumma inni asaluka khaira hâzihil lailati fathaha wa nasraha wa nûraha wa barkataha wa hudaha wa aûzubika min sharri-ma fîha wa sharri ma badaha.

O Allâh! I beg of Thee the good of this night, the victory thereof, the help thereof; and light thereof, the blessings thereof: and the guidance thereof; and I seek refuge in Thee from the evil that be therein, and the evil that be thereafter (in the evening).

20

At the Rising of The Sun

اَلْحَـمْدُ لِلّٰهِ الَّذِىٓ اَقَالَنَا يَوْمَنَا هٰذَا وَلَمْ يُهْلِكْنَا بِذُنُوْبِنَا.

Alhamdu lil lâhil lazi aqalana yaumana hâza wa lam yuhlikna bi-zunûbina.

All praise be to Him, Who excused us this day and did not destroy us on account of our misdeeds.

21

At the Call of Evening Prayer

اَللّٰهُمَّ اِنَّ هٰذَا اِقْبَالُ لَيْلِكَ وَاِدْبَارُ نَهَارِكَ وَاَصْوَاتُ دُعَآئِكَ فَاغْفِرْلِىْ.

Allâhumma inna hâza iqbalu lailika wa idbaru naharika wa aswâtu du'âika faghfirlî.

O Allâh! This is the hour of the advent of 'My night, and the departure of Thy day, and the sounds of Thy heralds, so grant me forgiveness.

22

بِسْمِ اللّٰهِ الَّذِىْ لَا يَضُرُّ مَعَ اسْمِهِ شَىْءٌ فِى الْاَرْضِ وَلَا فِى السَّمَآءِ وَهُوَ السَّمِيْعُ الْعَلِيْمُ

Bismillâhil-lazi la yadhurru ma-a-ismihi shai-un fil-ardhi wala fis-sama-i wa huwas samiul alîm.

In the name of Allâh, He with Whose name nothing; either on the earth or in the sky, can do any harm. He is the Best Hearer and Knower.

23

At the Time of Going to Bed

اَللّٰهُمَّ قِنِىْ عَذَابَكَ يَوْمَ تَبْعَثُ عِبَادَكَ.

Allâhummaqini azabaka yauma tab-asu ibadaka.

O Allâh! Save me from the pangs of the Day of Resurrection.

24

اَللّٰهُمَّ بِاسْمِكَ اَمُوْتُ وَاَحْيٰى

Allâhumma bismika amûtu wa ahya.

O Allâh! In Thy name do I die and live.

25

At the Time of Awakening

اَلْحَمْدُ لِلّٰهِ الَّذِيْ اَحْيَانَا بَعْدَ مَا اَمَاتَنَا وَ اِلَيْهِ النُّشُوْرُ

Alhamdu lil lâhil lazi ahyâna bâda ma amatana wa ilaihin-nushûru.

All praise to Allâh, He Who revived us to life after giving us death, and to Him we shall have to return.

26

اَعُوْذُ بِكَلِمَاتِ اللّٰهِ التَّامَّةِ مِنْ غَضَبِهٖ وَعَقَابِهٖ وَشَرِّ عِبَادِهٖ وَمِنْ هَمَزَاتِ الشَّيَاطِيْنِ وَاَنْ يَّحْضُرُوْنِ

Aûzu bi kalimatil lahit tâmmati min ghadhabihî wa iqabihî wa sharri ibadihi wa min hama-zatish shayatîni wa any yahdhurûn.

I seek refuge, through the complete words of Allâh, from His anger, His punishment, and the mischief of His men, and the evil suggestions of the devils, lest they should come to me.

27

At Tahajjud

اَللّٰهُمَّ لَكَ الْحَمْدُ اَنْتَ قَيِّمُ السَّمٰوٰتِ وَالْاَرْضِ وَ مَنْ

فِيْهِنَّ وَلَكَ الْحَمْدُ اَنْتَ نُوْرُ السَّمٰوٰتِ وَالْاَرْضِ

وَمَنْ فِيْهِنَّ وَلَكَ الْحَمْدُ اَنْتَ مَلِكُ السَّمٰوٰتِ

وَالْاَرْضِ وَمَنْ فِيْهِنَّ اَنْتَ الْحَقُّ وَعْدُكَ حَقٌّ

وَّلِقَآؤُكَ حَقٌّ وَّقَوْلُكَ حَقٌّ وَّالْجَنَّةُ حَقٌّ وَّالنَّارُ حَقٌّ

وَّالنَّبِيُّوْنَ حَقٌّ وَّ مُحَمَّدٌ حَقٌّ وَّالسَّاعَةُ حَقٌّ اَللّٰهُمَّ

لَكَ اَسْلَمْتُ وَبِكَ اٰمَنْتُ وَعَلَيْكَ تَوَكَّلْتُ وَاِلَيْكَ اَنَبْتُ

وَبِكَ خَاصَمْتُ وَاِلَيْكَ حَاكَمْتُ فَاغْفِرْلِى مَا قَدَّمْتُ

وَمَا اَخَّرْتُ وَمَا اَسْرَرْتُ وَمَا اَعْلَنْتُ وَمَا اَنْتَ اَعْلَمُ

بِهٖ مِنِّى اَنْتَ الْمُقَدِّمُ وَاَنْتَ الْمُؤَخِّرُ لَا اِلٰهَ اِلَّاۤ اَنْتَ

وَلَاۤ اِلٰهَ غَيْرُكَ.

*Allâhumma lakal hamdu anta qayiimus-
samawati wal ardhi wa man fi hinna wa lakal
Hamdu anta nûrus-samawati wal ardhi wa
man fi hinna wa lakal hamdu anta malikus-
samawati wal ardhi wa man fi hinna antal
haqqu wâduka haqqun wa liqa-uka haqqun
wa Qauluka haqqun wal jannatu haqqun
wan naru haqqun wan nabiyûna haqqun wa
Muhammadun haqqun was sa-atu haqqun
allâhumma laka aslamtu wa bika âmantu wa
alaika tawakkaltu wa ilaika anabtu wa bika
khasamtu wa ilaika hakamtu faghfirli ma
qaddamtu wa ma akhkhartu wa ma asrartu
wa ma âlantu wa ma anta âlamu bihi minni*

*antal muqaddimu wa antal muakhkhiru la
ilâha illa anta wa la ilaha ghairuka.*

O Allâh! Praise be to Thee, Thou art
the Guardian of the Heavens and the
earth, and of those that are therein. Praise
be to Thee, Thou art the light of the
heavens and the earth and of those that
are therein. Unto Thee belongeth the
praise, Thou art the King of the heavens
and the earth, and of those that are
therein. Thou art True, True is Thy
promise, True is our meeting with Thee,
True is Thy word, True is heaven, and
True is hell, True are the prophets, True
is Muhammad, and True is the Hour of
Judgement. O Allâh! Unto Thee do I
surrender: In Thee I have faith; upon
Thee do I rely; unto Thee do I turn. With
Thy help do I contend; and unto Thee do
I seek judgement. So forgive me for that
which I expedite. And that which I defer,

and that which I conceal. And that which I reveal. And also for that (Sin) of mine whereof Thou art better aware than I. Thou art the Expediter and Thou art the Deferer. There is no god other than Thee.

28

At the time of Entering and Coming Out of the Closet.

بِسْمِ اللهِ اللّٰهُمَّ اِنِّى اَعُوْذُ بِكَ مِنَ الْخُبُثِ وَالْخَبَآئِثِ

Bismillâhi allâhumma inni aûzubika minal khubusi wal khaba-isi.

In the name of Allâh. O Allâh! I seek refuge in Thee from the foul male and female devils.

غُفْرَانَكَ اَلْحَمْدُ لِلّٰهِ الَّذِىْ اَذْهَبَ عَنِّىَ الْاَذَىٰ وَعَافَانِى

Ghufranaka al-hamdu lil-lâ-hil lazi azhaba annil azâ wa a-fâni.

(I ask) Thy pardon. Praise be to Allâh Who relieved me from the suffering and gave me health.

29

At the Beginning of Wuzu (Ablution)

اَللّٰهُمَّ اِنّىِّ اَعُوْذُ بِكَ مِنْ هَمَزَاتِ الشَّيَاطِيْنِ وَ اَعُوْذُ
بِكَ رَبِّ اَنْ يَّحْضُرُوْنَ.

Allâh humma inni aûzubika min hamazatish shayatîni wa aûzubika Rabbi any-yadhurûn.

O Allâh! Verily, I seek refuge in Thee from the evil suggestions of the devils, and I seek refuge in Thee, lest they should come to me.

30

بِسْمِ اللّٰهِ الْعَظِيْمِ وَالْحَمْدُ لِلّٰهِ عَلٰى دِيْنِ الْاِسْلَامِ

Bismilla-hil azimi wal hamdu lil lâhi ala dinil Islam.

In the name of Allâh, the exalted, and praise be to Him for (keeping me faithful) to the religion to Islam.

31

اَللّٰهُمَّ اغْفِرْلِى ذَنبِى وَوَسِّعْ لِى فِى دَارِى وَبَارِكْ لِى فِى رِزْقِى.

Allâhummagh firlî zambî wa wassi lî fî dari wa barik lî fî rizqi.

O Allâh! Grant me forgiveness for my sins, grant me expansion in my house, and bless my livelihood.

32

At the Time of Washing Hands

اَللّٰهُمَّ اِنِّى اَسْئَلُكَ الْيُمْنَ وَالْبَرَكَةَ وَاَعُوذُ بِكَ مِنَ الشُّؤْمِ وَالْهَلاكَةِ.

Allâh humma inni asalukal yumna wal

barkata wa aûzubika minash shûmi wal
halakati.

O Allâh! I ask of Thee good fortune
and blessing, and seek refuge in. Thee
from misfortune and destruction.

33
At the Time of Gargling

اَللّٰهُمَّ اَعِنِّیْ عَلٰی تِلَاوَةِ كِتَابِكَ وَكَثْرَةِ
الذِّكْرِلَكَ وَالشُّكْرِ لَكَ.

Allâhumma a'ainni ala tilawati kitabika
wa kasratiz zikri laka wash shukri laka.

O Allâh! Help me in the recitation of
'Thy Book, and in remembering Thee
most, and in offering Thee thanks.

34
At the Time of Pouring Water
in Nostrils

اَللّٰهُمَّ ارْحِنِیْ رَائِحَةَ الْجَنَّةِ وَاَنْتَ عَنِّیْ رَاضٍ.

Allâh humma arihni ra-ihatal jannati wa anta anni radhin.

O Allâh! Comfort me with the smell of Heaven, and under the circumstances that Thou art pleased with me.

35
While Snuffing Nose

اَللّٰهُمَّ اَعُوْذُ بِكَ مِنْ رَوَآئِحِ النَّارِ وَمِنْ سُوْءِ الدَّارِ

Allâhumma aûzubika min rawâ-ihin nari wamin sû-iddari.

O Allâh! I seek refuge in Thee from the smell of the fire. (Of the Hell) and from the disgrace of the abode.

36
While Washing Face

اَللّٰهُمَّ بَيِّضْ وَجْهِیْ یَوْمَ تَبْیَضُّ وُجُوْهُ اَوْلِیَآئِكَ وَ لَا تُسَوِّدْ وَجْهِیْ یَوْمَ تَسْوَدُّ وُجُوْهُ اَعْدَآئِكَ

Allâhumma biyyidh waj hi yauma tabyadhdhu wu juhu auliaika wala tusawwid wajhi yauma taswaddu wu juhu âdâika.

O Allâh! Brighten my face on the day when Thou wouldst brighten the faces of those who are dear to Thee, and do not blacken my face on the day when Thou wouldst blacken the faces of Thy foes.

37

While Washing Right Hand to the Elbow

اَللّٰهُمَّ اَعْطِنِیْ كِتَابِیْ بِيَمِیْنِی وَ حَاسِبْنِیْ حِسَابًا يَّسِيْرًا

Allâhumma âtini kitabi biyamîni wa hasibni hisabany yasîra

O Allâh! Give me the record of my deeds in my right hand and subject me to an easy judgement.

38
While Washing Left Hand to the Elbow

اَللّٰهُمَّ اِنِّىْ اَعُوْذُ بِكَ اَنْ تُعْطِيَنِىْ كِتَابِىْ بِشِمَالِىْ اَوْ مِنْ وَّرَآءِ ظَهْرِىْ

Allâhumma inni aûzubika an tutiyani kitabi bi-shimali au-minw wara-i Zahari.

O Allâh! I seek refuge in Thee that I may be given the record of my deeds in my left hand or from behind my back.

39
While Wiping Head

اَللّٰهُمَّ اَظِلِّنِىْ تَحْتَ ظِلِّ عَرْشِكَ يَوْمَ لَا ظِلَّ اِلَّا ظِلُّ عَرْشِكَ

Allâhumma azillini tahta zilli arshika yauma la zilla illa zilla arshika.

O Allâh! Give me the shade of shelter under Thy Throne, on the day when there will be no shade other than the shade of Thy Throne.

40
While Wiping Ears

اَللّٰهُمَّ اجْعَلْنِىْ مِنَ الَّذِيْنَ يَسْتَمِعُوْنَ الْقَوْلَ فَيَتَّبِعُوْنَ أَحْسَنَهٗ اَللّٰهُمَّ اَسْمِعْنِىْ مُنَادِىَ الْجَنَّةِ مَعَ الْاَبْرَارِ.

Allâhummaj 'alni minal lazîna yas tami'u-nal qaula fa yattabi-'una ahsanahu alla humma asm'ini muna-diyal jannati ma al abrar.

O Allâh! Make me as one of those who listen to an utterance and follow what is best in it. O Allâh! Make me listen to the pronounce ment of the Heaven along with the virtuous people.

41
While Wiping Neck

اَللّٰهُمَّ فُكَّ رَقَبَتِىْ مِنَ النَّارِ وَ اَعُوْذُبِكَ مِنَ السَّلَاسِلِ وَالْاَغْلَالِ.

Allâh humma fukka raqabati minan nari wa aûzubika minas salasili wal aghlali.

O Allâh! Take my neck off from the hell fire and I seek Thy refuge from the fetters and shackles.

42
While Washing Right Foot

اَللّٰهُمَّ ثَبِّتْ قَدَمَىَّ عَلٰى صِرَاطِكَ الْمُسْتَقِيْمِ.

Allâhumma sabbit qadamay-ya'ala siratikal-mustaqîm.

O Allâh! Let my feet stick to the right path.

43
While Washing Left Foot

اَللّٰهُمَّ اِنِّىْ اَعُوْذُ بِكَ اَنْ تَزِلَّ قَدَمَىَّ عَلَى الصِّرَاطِ يَوْمَ تَزِلُّ اَقْدَامُ الْمُنَافِقِيْنَ فِى النَّارِ

Allâhumma inni aûzubika an tazilla qadamayya alas sirati yauma tazillu aqdamul munafiqîna finnar.

O Allâh! I seek Thy refuge that my feet slip on the bridge on the day when the feet of the hypocrites slip in hell.

44

At the End of Wuzu

اَشْهَدُ اَنْ لَّا اِلٰهَ اِلَّا اللّٰهُ وَحْدَهُ لَاشَرِيْكَ لَهُ وَاَشْهَدُ اَنَّ مُحَمَّدًا عَبْدُهُ وَرَسُوْلُهُ اَللّٰهُمَّ اجْعَلْنِىْ مِنَ التَّوَّابِيْنَ وَاجْعَلْنِىْ مِنَ الْمُتَطَهِّرِيْنَ وَاجْعَلْنِىْ مِنْ عِبَادِكَ الصّٰلِحِيْنَ

Ash-hadu al lâ ilaha illal lahu wahdahu la sharîka lahu wa ash hadu anna Muham-madan abduhu wa rasûluhu. Alla hummaj alni minat tawwabîna waj alni min al-muta-tahhirîna wajalni min ibadikas sualihîn.

I testify that there is no god besides

Allâh; He is alone, He has no partner; and I (further) testify that Muhammad is indeed His bondsman and apostle. O Allâh! Make me of those who are repentant; and make me of those who are purified and make me of those who are Thy virtuous servants.

45
On Hearing Adhan

اَللّٰهُمَّ رَبَّ هٰذِهِ الدَّعْوَةِ التَّامَّةِ وَالصَّلٰوةِ الْقَائِمَةِ اٰتِ
مُحَمَّدَ نِ الْوَسِيلَةَ وَالْفَضِيلَةَ وَالدَّرَجَةَ الرَّفِيعَةَ
وَابْعَثْهُ مَقَامًا مَّحْمُودًا نِ الَّذِىْ وَعَدْتَّهُ وَارْزُقْنَا
شَفَاعَتَهُ يَوْمَ الْقِيَامَةِ اِنَّكَ لَا تُخْلِفُ الْمِيْعَادَ

Allâhumma rabba hazihid dawatit tâmmati was salatil qaimati ati Muhammada nil wasilata wal fadhîlata wad darajatar rafi'ata wab as-hu maqamam mahmûda nil lazi wa attahu war zuqna shafa'atahu yaumal qiyamati innaka la tukhliful mî'yâd.

Allâh! Lord of this perfect call and of the salat to be offered presently, vouchsafe Muhammad the way of approach unto Thee, and also eminence, and elevate him to the glorious position which Thou hast promised him, and afford us his intercession on the Day of Judgement and Thou goest not back on Thy promise.

46
While Entering Mosque

While entering the mosque one should plant one's right foot first and then the left, and along with Darud offer the following prayer;

اَللّٰهُمَّ افْتَحْ لِىْ اَبْوَابَ رَحْمَتِكَ

Allâhummaf tahli abwâba rahmatika

Allâh! Open unto me the gates of Thy Mercy.

47
While Stepping Out of Mosque

After reciting Darud one should utter these words.

اَللّٰهُمَّ اِنِّىْ اَسْئَلُكَ مِنْ فَضْلِكَ

Allâhumma inni asaluka min Fazlika.

O Allâh! I beg of Thee Thy bounty.

48
After Morning and Evening Prayers

The following Supplication Should be made after Morning and Evening Prayers.

اَللّٰهُمَّ اَجِرْنِىْ مِنَ النَّارِ

Allâhumma ajirni minan nari.

O Allâh! Protect me against the fire (of Hell).

49
After Offering Forenoon Prayer

اَللّٰهُمَّ بِكَ أُحَاوِلُ وَبِكَ أُصَاوِلُ وَبِكَ أُقَاتِلُ

Allâhumma bika ohawilu wa bika usawilu wa bika oqatilu

O Allâh! With Thy help do I strive, with Thy help do I assail, and with Thy help do I battle.

50
Qunut Nazilah

It is reported by authentic narrators that the Holy Prophet recited supplication known as *Qunut Nazilah* in the Morning Prayer. The procedure is that the Imam alongwith his followers in the second rakat stands erect after ruku keeping their arms on their sides. The Imam recites this prayer and the followers say Aamin at the proper juncture and then all fall in prostration.

اَللّٰهُمَّ اهْدِنَا فِيْمَنْ هَدَيْتَ وَعَافِنَا فِىْ مَنْ عَافَيْتَ وَ
تَوَلَّنَا فِىْ مَنْ تَوَلَّيْتَ وَبَارِكْ لَنَا فِىْ مَاۤ اَعْطَيْتَ وَقِنَا
شَرَّمَا قَضَيْتَ فَاِنَّكَ تَقْضِىْ وَلَا يُقْضٰى عَلَيْكَ اِنَّهٗ
لَايَذِلُّ مَنْ وَّالَيْتَ وَلَا يَعِزُّ مَنْ عَادَيْتَ تَبَارَكْتَ رَبَّنَا
وَتَعَالَيْتَ نَسْتَغْفِرُكَ وَنَتُوْبُ اِلَيْكَ وَصَلَّ اللّٰهُ عَلَى
النَّبِىِّ الْكَرِيْمِ اَللّٰهُمَّ اغْفِرْلَنَا وَلِلْمُؤْمِنِيْنَ وَالْمُؤْمِنَاتِ
وَالْمُسْلِمِيْنَ وَالْمُسْلِمَاتِ وَاَلِّفْ بَيْنَ قُلُوْبِهِمْ
وَاَصْلِحْ ذَاتَ بَيْنِهِمْ وَانْصُرْهُمْ عَلٰى عَدُوِّكَ
وَعَدُوِّهِمْ اَللّٰهُمَّ قَاتِلِ الْكَفَرَةَ الَّذِيْنَ يَجْحَدُوْنَ اٰيٰتِكَ
وَيُكَذِّبُوْنَ رُسُلَكَ وَيَصُدُّوْنَ عَنْ سَبِيْلِكَ وَيُقَاتِلُوْنَ
اَوْلِيَآئَكَ اَللّٰهُمَّ انْصُرِ الْاِسْلَامَ وَ الْمُسْلِمِيْنَ وَاخْذُلْ
اَعْدَآئَهُمُ الْيَهُوْدَ وَالنَّصٰرٰى وَالْمُشْرِكِيْنَ اَللّٰهُمَّ
شَتِّتْ شَمْلَهُمْ وَمَزِّقْ جَمْعَهُمْ وَخَالِفْ بَيْنَ كَلِمَتِهِمْ

وَامْحُ اٰثَارَهُمْ وَاقْطَعْ دَابِرَهُمْ وَاَنْزِلْ بِهِمْ بَأْسَكَ

الَّذِىْ لَاتَرُدُّهُ عَنِ الْقَوْمِ الْمُجْرِمِيْنَ اَللّٰهُمَّ اَهْلِكْهُمْ

كَمَآ اَهْلَكْتَ عَادًا وَّثَمُوْدَ اَللّٰهُمَّ خُذْهُمْ اَخْذَ عَزِيْزٍ

مُّقْتَدِرٌ

Allâh hummahdina fi man hadaita wa
âfina fi man afaita watawallana fi man
tawallaita wa barik lana fi ma ataita waqina
sharra ma qadhaita fa innaka taqdhi wala
yuqdha alaika innahu la yazillu man wa laita
wala ya izzu man âdaita tabarakta rabbana
wata 'alaita nas taghfiruka wa natubu ilaika
wa sallallâhu alan nabiyil karim
allâhummagh-fir lana wa lil muminina wal
muminati wal muslimina wal muslimati wa-
allif baina qulubihim wa aslih zata bainihim
wansurhum ala adûwwika wa adûwwihim
allâhumma qatilil kafaratal lazina yajhadûna
âyatika wa yukazzibûna rusulaka wa
yasudduna 'an sabîlika wa yuqatiluna aulia
aka allâhummansuril islama wal muslimîna

wakhzul Aa-da-ahumul yahuda wan nasâra wal mushrikîna alla humma shattit shamlahum wa mazziq jam'ahum wa kahlif baina kalimatihim wamhu asârahum waqta dabirahum wa anzil bihim bâsakal lazi la tarud-duhu anil qaumil mujrimîn allahumma ahlik-hum kama ahlakta adan wa Samûd, allahumma khuzhum akhza Azizim muqtadir.

O Allâh! Guide us amongst those whom Thou hast guided aright and preserve us amongst those whom Thou hast preserved. Take us for a friend amongst those whom Thou hast taken for friends. Bless us in that which Thou hast bestowed upon us. Guard us from the evil of that which Thou hast ordained, for it is Thou Who ordainest, and none can ordain aught against Thee. Indeed! Never is he abased whom Thou takest as a friend, and none is respected whom Thou takest as a foe. Blessed art

Thou, our lord and Exalted. We ask repentance from Thee and turn to Thee; and shower Thy blessings on the Merciful Prophet O Allâh! Grant forgiveness to us and to the faithful males and females, Muslims-men and women. O Allâh! Bring affection (for one another) in their hearts; and bring reconciliation among them, Grant them victory against Thy foes and against their foes. O Allâh! Bring destruction to the unbelievers those who reject Thy words and disbelieve Thy messengers, and dissuade (people) from Thy path. And fight against Thy friends, O Allâh! Help Islam and the Muslims and leave alone their enemies helpless and friendless; the Jews and the Christians, and the Polytheists. Allâh! Dissolve their unity, rip apart their integration. Let there be dissension amongst them; obliterate their trace; Eradicate their roots; and let fall such a terrible calamity upon them as does not avert from the wrong-doers. O Allâh! Destroy them as Thou destroyed the Aad and the Thamud. O Allâh hold them in a grip which befits Thy power and dominance.

51

At the Conclusion of the prayer, one should recite, أَسْتَغْفِرُاللهَ

Astaghfirullâh (I seek forgiveness from Allâh) thrice an then make this supplication:

اَللَّهُـمَّ أَنْـتَ السَّلَامُ وَمِـنْكَ السَّلَامُ حَيِّـنَا رَبَّـنَا بِالسَّلَامِ وَأَدْخِـلْنَا دَارَالسَّلَامِ تَبَارَكْتَ يَا ذَالْجَلَالِ وَالْإِكْرَامِ سَمِعْنَا وَأَطَعْنَا غُفْرَانَكَ رَبَّنَا وَإِلَيْكَ الْمَصِيْرُ

Allâhumma antas salamu wa minkas salamu hayyina rabbana bissa-lami wa ad khilna darassalam tabaraka ya Zaljalali wal ikram, samina wa atana ghufranaka rabbana wa ilaikal masîr.

O Allâh! Thou art the Author of Peace and from Thee comes Peace; and Peace returns towards Thee. Keep us alive with peace, and let us enter the House of Peace. Blessed and Exalted art Thou O Lord of Glory and Honour! (Our Lords!) Hear us and grant us pardon; to Thee is (our) return.

After Witr one should recite the words:

سُبْحَانَ الْمَلِكِ الْقُدُّوسِ

Subhanal Malikil Quddus. (Glory be to the King, the Holy). To be recited thrice.

One should recite سُبْحَانَ اللّٰهِ
Subhan Allâh (Glory be to Allâh)
Thirty-three times.

Alhamdulillah اَلْحَمْدُ لِلّٰهِ

(Praise be to Allâh)

Thirty-three times, and اللّٰهُ اَكْبَرُ

Allâhu Akbar (Allâh is Great) Thirty four times after every prayer.

52
At the Time of Breaking Fast

اَللّٰهُمَّ لَكَ صُمْتُ وَعَلٰى رِزْقِكَ اَفْطَرْتُ.

Allâhumma laka sumtu wa 'ala rizqika aftartu.

O Allâh! It is for Thee I observe fast and it is with Thrine blessing that I break it.

53
After Breaking Fast

ذَهَبَ الظَّمَآءُ وَابْتَلَّتِ الْعُرُوْقُ وَثَبَتَ الْاَجْرُ اِنْ شَآءَ اللّٰهُ تَعَالٰى

Zahabazzamao wabtallatil urûqu wa sabatal ajru insha Allâhu ta-'ala

No more was the thirst, moistened were the veins, and the reward became due, the Lord so willed.

54

While Breaking the Fast at the Table of Another Person

أَفْطَرَ عِنْدَكُمُ الصَّآئِمُونَ وَأَكَلَ طَعَامَكُمُ الْأَبْرَارُ وَصَلَّتْ عَلَيْكُمُ الْمَلَئِكَةُ.

Aftara indakumus-sa-imuna wa akala ta amakumul abraru wa sallat alaikumul malaikatu

May the observers of fast break it at your (table) and the pious take meals at your (house) and angels beg mercy for you.

55

اَللّٰهُمَّ بَارِكْ لَهُمْ فِيمَا رَزَقْتَهُمْ وَاغْفِرْلَهُمْ وَارْحَمْهُمْ

Allâhumma barik lahum fîma razaqtahum waghfir lahum war-hamhum.

O Allâh! Bless their livelihood that Thou gavest them; grant them pardon and grant them mercy.

56
Supplication in Taraweeh

سُبْحَانَ ذِى الْمُلْكِ وَالْمَلَكُوْتِ سُبْحَانَ ذِى الْعِزَّةِ
وَالْعَظَمَةِ وَالْهَيْبَةِ وَالْقُدْرَةِ وَالْكِبْرِيَآءِ وَالْجَبَرُوْتِ
سُبْحَانَ الْمَلِكِ الْحَيِّ الَّذِىْ لَايَنَامُ وَلَا يَمُوْتُ
سُبُّوْحٌ قُدُّوْسٌ رَبُّنَا وَرَبُّ الْمَلٰئِكَةِ وَالرُّوْحِ اَللّٰهُمَّ
اَجِرْنَا مِنَ النَّارِ يَا مُجِيْرُ يَا مُجِيْرُ يَا مُجِيْرُ

Subhana zil-mulki wal malakûti subhana zil izzati wal azmati wal haibati wal qudrati wal kibriya-i wal jabarûti subhanal maliki hayyil-lazi la yanamu wala yamûtu subbûhun quddûsun rabbuna wa rabbul mala-ikati warrûh allahumma ajirna minannari ya Mujîru ya Mujîru ya Mujîr.

Glory be to the Master of this world and that of the Heaven. Glory be to the Possessor of honour, greatness, and dominion, majesty and might. Glory be to the Ever-living Sovereign Who neither sleeps nor dies. O All Glorious All Holy One. Our Lord and Lord of the Angels, and the soul. O Allâh! Save us.

57
An Important Supplication in Pilgrimage

This supplication is made after donning the *Ihram* (Pilgrimage dress)

لَبَّيْكَ اللّٰهُمَّ لَبَّيْكَ لَبَّيْكَ لَا شَرِيكَ لَكَ لَبَّيْكَ إِنَّ الْحَمْدَ وَالنِّعْمَةَ لَكَ وَالْمُلْكَ لَا شَرِيكَ لَكَ.

Labbaika allahumma labbaik labbaika la sharika laka labbaik innal hamda wannimata laka wal mulka la sharika laka.

Here I am at Thy service, O Allâh!

am at Thy Service. No partner hast Thou. Here I am at Thy service. Verily unto Thee belong the praise and the bounty and also the sovereignty. No partner has Thou.

58
At the Time of Beginning Meal

بِسْمِ اللّٰهِ وَعَلٰى بَرَكَةِ اللّٰهِ.

Bismillâhi wa'ala barakatillah

In the name of Allâh and with the blessings of Allâh.

59
At the Finishing of Meal

اَلْحَمْدُ لِلّٰهِ الَّذِىْ اَطْعَمَنَا وَسَقَانَا وَجَعَلَنَا مِنَ الْمُسْلِمِيْنَ.

Al hamdu lil lâhil lazi atamana wa saqana waja-'alana minal muslimîn.

Praise be to Allâh Who fed us and gave us drink and made us Muslims.

60
While Dinning at the Table
of Other Person

اَللّٰهُمَّ اَطْعِمْ مَنْ اَطْعَمَنِیْ وَاسْقِ مَنْ سَقَانِیْ

Allâhumma at'im man at'amani wasqi man saqâni

O Allâh! Feed him who fed me and give him drink who gave me drink.

61
After Taking Milk

اَللّٰهُمَّ بَارِكْ لَنَا فِيْهِ وَزِدْنَا مِنْهُ

Allâhumma bârik lana fîhi wa zidna minhu.

O Allâh! Bless us with it and increase it for us.

62
At the Time of Donning
a New Garment

اَلْحَمْدُ لِلّٰهِ الَّذِیْ كَسَانِیْ مَآ اُوَارِیْ بِهٖ عَوْرَتِیْ

وَاَتَجَمَّلُ بِهِ فِى حَيَاتِى

Alhamdu lil lâhil lazi kasani ma uwari
bihi aurati wa ata jammalu behi fi hayatî.

Praise be to Allâh, Who clad me with
that wherewith I cover my shame and
wherewith I adorn myself in my life.

63

Supplication for Istikharah

When anyone intends to do anything,
let him offer two rak'at of unobligatory
prayer, and then recite:

اَللّٰهُمَّ اِنِّى اَسْتَخِيْرُكَ بِعِلْمِكَ وَاَسْتَقْدِرُكَ بِقُدْرَتِكَ

وَاَسْئَلُكَ مِنْ فَضْلِكَ الْعَظِيْمِ ۖ فَاِنَّكَ تَقْدِرُ وَلَاۤ اَقْدِرُ

وَتَعْلَمُ وَلَاۤ اَعْلَمُ وَاَنْتَ عَلَّامُ الْغُيُوْبِ اَللّٰهُمَّ اِنْ كُنْتَ

تَعْلَمُ اِنَّ هٰذَا الْاَمْرَ خَيْرٌ لِّى فِى دِيْنِى وَمَعَاشِى

وَعَاقِبَةِ اَمْرِى فَاقْدِرْهُ لِى وَيَسِّرْهُ لِى ثُمَّ بَارِكْ لِى

فِيهِ وَإِنْ كُنْتَ تَعْلَمُ اِنَّ هٰذَا الْاَمْرَشَرٌّ لِّى فِى دِينِى

وَمَعَاشِى وَعَاقِبَةِ اَمْرِى فَاصْرِفْهُ عَنِّى وَاصْرِفْنِى

عَنْهُ وَاقْدِرْلِىَ الْخَيْرَ حَيْثُ كَانَ ثُمَّ اَرْضِنِى بِهِ

Allâhumma inni astakhiruka bi ilmika wa astaqdiruka biqudratika wa asaluka min fadhlikal azîmi. Fa innaka taqdiru wala aqdiru wa talamu wala alamu wa anta 'allamul ghuyûbi. Allâhumma in kunta talamu anna hâzal amra khairul lî fî dînî wa ma'ashî wa âqibati amri faqdirhu lî wa yassirhu lî summa bârik lî fîhi wa in kunta tâlamu anna hâzal amra sharrul lî fî dîni wa ma'ashi wa âqibati amri fasrifhu anni wasrifni anhu waqdir liyal khaira haisu kâna summa ardhini bihi.

O Allâh! I beg Thee the Good through Thy knowledge and ability; through Thy power and beg (Thy favours) out of Thine infinite bounty; for Thou hast power, I have none. Thou knowest, I

56

know not and Thou art the Great knower of things hidden. O Allâh! If in Thy knowledge this matter be good for my faith, for my livelihood and for the consequences of my affairs, then ordain it for me and bless me therein; but if in Thy knowledge this matter be bad for my faith, for my livelihood and for the consequences of my affairs, then turn it away from me and turn me away therefrom and ordain for me the good wherever it be and cause me to be pleased therewith.

64

Seeking Divine Help in the Memorisation of the Holy Qur'an

Whoever intends to memorise the Holy Qur'an, he should on a Friday night wake up in the third part of the night or midnight and if that is not possible, even in the earlier part of the night and offer four rak'ats. In the first rak'at he should recite Surah *Fatiha* and *Ya'sîn,* in the second one *Fatiha* and *Dukhân,* in the third one *Fatiha* and Al-Sajdah, in 'the fourth one *Fatiha* and *Al-Mulk.*

At the conclusion of this prayer, he should glorify Allâh and shower blessings in the form of Darûd upon Muhammad (may the peace of Allâh be upon him) and all other apostles of the Lord, and beg pardon from Him for all the Muslims, male and female, and for those who are their predecessors in faith. Then he should make the following supplication to the Lord with the firm conviction that it will be granted:

اَللّٰهُمَّ ارْحَمْنِىْ بِتَرْكِ الْمَعَاصِىْ اَبَدًا مَّآ اَبْقَيْتَنِىْ

وَارْحَمْنِىْ اَنْ تَكَلَّفَ مَا لَا يُعْنِيْنِىْ وَارْزُقْنِىْ حُسْنَ

النَّظَرِ فِيمَا يُرْضِيكَ عَنِّى اَللَّهُمَّ بَدِيعَ السَّمٰوٰتِ
وَالْأَرْضِ ذَالْجَلَالِ وَالْإِكْرَامِ وَالْعِزَّةِ الَّتِى لَاتُرَامُ
اَسْئَلُكَ يَا اَللّٰهُ يَا رَحْمٰنُ بِجَلَالِكَ وَنُورِ وَجْهِكَ اَنْ
تُلْزِمَ قَلْبِى حِفْظَ كِتَابِكَ كَمَا عَلَّمْتَنِى وَارْزُقْنِى اَنْ
اَقْرَئَهُ عَلَى النَّحْوِ الَّذِى يُرْضِيكَ عَنِّى اَللَّهُمَّ بَدِيعَ
السَّمٰوٰتِ وَالْأَرْضِ ذَالْجَلَالِ وَالْإِكْرَامِ وَالْعِزَّةِالَّتِى
لَا تُرَامُ اَسْئَلُكَ يَا اَللّٰـهُ يَا رَحْمٰنُ بِجَلَالِكَ وَنُورِ
وَجْهِكَ اَنْ تُنَوِّرَ بِكَ بَصَرِى وَاَنْ تُطْلِقَ بِهِ لِسَانِى
وَاَنْ تُفَرِّجَ بِهِ عَنْ قَلْبِى وَاَنْ تَشْرَحَ بِهِ صَدْرِى وَ اَنْ
تَغْسِلَ بِهِ بَدَنِى فَاِنَّهُ لَا يُعِيْنُنِى عَلَى الْحَقِّ غَيْرُكَ
وَلَا يُؤْتِيْهِ اِلَّا اَنْتَ وَلَا حَوْلَ وَلَا قُوَّةَ اِلَّا بِاللّٰهِ الْعَلِّى
الْعَظِيمِه

Allâhumma-r hamni bi tarkil ma'asî
abadam ma abqaitani warhamni an takallafa
mala yaunini warzuqni husnan nazari fima

*yurdhika anni allahumma badi as-samawati
wal ardhi zaljalali wal ikrami wal izzatil lati
la turamu asaluka ya allahu ya rahmanu be
jalalika wa nûri wajhika an tulzima qalbi
hifza kitabika kama allamtani war zuqni an
aqra-ahu alannahwil lazi yurdhika anni
allahumma badi assamawati walardhi
zaljalali walikram wal izzatillati la turamu
asaluka ya allahu ya rahmanu bi jalalika wa
nûri wajhika an tunawwira bika basari wa an
tutliqa bihi lisani wa an tufarrija bihi an qalbi
wa an tashraha bihi sadri wa an taghsila bihi
badani fa innahu la yuînuni alal haqqi
ghairuka wala yutîhi illa anta wa la haula
wala quwwata illa billahil aliyil azîm.*

O Allâh! Be Thou Gracious unto me
by enabling me to give up sins
altogether. As long as Thou grantest me
life and hast mercy upon me, lest I should
concern myself with aught which is of no
consequence to me; and vouchsafe me
the goodness of sight which will cause

Thee to be well pleased with me. O Allâh! Originator of the heavens and the earth; Lord of majesty, glory and of might incomprehensible! I beseech Thee, O Allâh, O Beneficent Lord. In the name of Thy Majesty and of the Light of Thy Countenance; to cause my heart to retain Thy Scripture even as Thou bast taught (if unto me). And grant that I may recite it in such a manner as will cause Thee to be well pleased with me. O Allâh! Originator of the heavens and the earth- Lord of Majesty, glory and of might incomprehensible! I beseech Thee, O Beneficent Lord! In the name of Thy Majesty and of the light of Thy countenance to illuminate my sight with My Scripture, to set free my tongue, to comfort my heart therewith to open my bosom therewith, and to wash my body therewith. For, indeed! None helps me in (the path of) truth besides Thee and favours me besides Thee. There is no strength nor power save in Allâh, the Exalted, the Magnificent.

65
For Greeting the Bride and the Bridegroom

بَارَكَ اللّٰـهُ لَكَ وَبَارَكَ اللّٰـهُ عَلَيْكَ وَجَمَعَ بَيْنَكُمَا فِىْ خَيْرٍ

Barakallahu laka wa barakallâhu alaika wa jamâ bainakuma fi khair.

May Allâh bless you and shower His blessing upon you twain and keep you in a happy union.

66
On Privacy in the First Night When the Spouse meet together

The husband should take hold of the forelock of his wife and make this supplication. It is also effective at the time of buying an animal.

اَللّٰهُمَّ اِنِّیْ اَسْئَلُكَ مِنْ خَيْرِهَا وَخَيْرِمَا جَبَلْتَهَا عَلَيْهِ

اَعُوْذُ بِكَ مِنْ شَرِّهَا وَشَرِّمَا جَبَلْتَهَا عَلَيْهِ

Allahumma inni asaluka min khairaha wa khairima jabaltaha alaihi aûzubika min sharriha wa sharrima jabaltaha alaihi.

O Allâh! I beg of Thee the Good of this (with) and the good of disposition wherewith thou hast created her and I ask refuge in Thee from her evil and from the evil of her disposition wherewith Thou hast created her.

67
At the Time of Sexual Intercourse

بِسْمِ اللّٰهِ اَللّٰهُمَّ جَنِّبْنَا الشَّيْطٰنَ وَجَنِّبِ الشَّيْطٰنَ مَارَزَقْتَنَا

Bismillâhi allahumma jannibnash shaitana wa janibish shaitana ma razaqtana.

In the name of Allâh. O Allâh! Guard us against Satan and cause Satan to keep off from what Thou vouchsafest us.

68
At the Time of Ejaculation of Sperm

اَللّٰهُمَّ لَا تَجْعَلْ لِلشَّيْطٰنِ فِيْمَا رَزَقْتَنِى نَصِيْبَاً

Allâhumma la taj'allish-shaitani fima razaqtani nasîba.

O Allâh! Let Satan not take any part of the chile which Thou hast destined for me.

69
While Bidding Good-Bye to Anybody

اَسْتَوْدِعُ اللّٰهَ دِيْنَكَ وَاَمَانَتَكَ وَخَوَاتِيْمَ عَمَلِكَ

Astaudi-ullaha dînaka wa amânataka wa
khawatîma 'amalika

Unto Allâh! Commend Thy faith, Thy
trust and the consequence of Thy work.

70
At the Time of Undertaking
a Journey

اَللّٰهُمَّ بِكَ اَصُوْلُ وَبِكَ اَحُوْلُ وَ بِكَ اَسِيْرُ

Allâhumma bika asulu wa bika ahulu wa
bika asîru

O Allâh! It is by Thy help that I do
assail and it is by Thy help that I move
and it is by Thy help that I walk.

71
At the Time of Riding

While riding a horse or boarding a
train or boarding a plane, one should
recite.

بِسْمِ اللّٰهِ

Bismillah (In the name of Allâh) and after having taken one's seat one should make the following supplication:

اَلْحَمْدُ لِلّٰهِ سُبْحَانَ الَّذِىْ سَخَّرَلَنَا هٰذَا وَمَاكُنَّا لَهُ

مُقْرِنِيْنَ ٥ وَاِنَّاۤاِلٰى رَبِّنَا لَمُنْقَلِبُوْنَ ٥

Alhamdu lil lahi subhanal lazi sakhkhara lana haza wama kunna lahu muqrinîna, wa inna ila rabbina la munqalibûn

Praise be to Allâh, Glory unto Him, who hath subjected this (vehicle...) for us, though we were unable to subdue it. Behold we are assuredly to return unto our Lord.

72
After having Set Out a Journey

اَللّٰهُمَّ هَوِّنْ عَلَيْنَا هٰذَا السَّفَرَ وَاطْوِعَنَّا بُعْدَهُ اَللّٰهُمَّ

أَنْتَ الصَّاحِبُ فِى السَّفَرِ وَالْخَلِيْفَةُ فِى الْاَهْلِ اَللّٰهُمَّ

إِنِّيْ اَعُوْذُ بِكَ مِنْ وَّعْتَاءِ السَّفَرِ وَكَابَةِ الْمَنْظَرِ وَسُوْءِ الْمُنْقَلَبِ فِى الْمَالِ وَالْاَهْلِ وَالْوَلَدِ

Allahumma haw-win 'alaina hazas safara watwi anna budahu allahumma antas sahibu fis safari wal khalifatu fil ahli allahumma inni aûzubika min-wa-sa-issafari wa ka-abatil manzari wa su-il munqalabi fil mali wal ahli wal waladi.

O Allâh! Make easy for us this journey of ours and roll up for us the distance thereof. O Allâh! Thou art our companion in this journey and guardian in (our) household. O Allâh! I seek refuge in 'Thee from the toil of this journey, from beholding a miserable sight and on ill return in my wealth, household and my children.

73
On Return from Journey

آئِبُوْنَ تَائِبُوْنَ عَابِدُوْنَ لِرَبِّنَا حَامِدُوْنَ

Aaibuna taibuna abiduna li rabbina hamidûna.

We are returners, penitents, worshippers and adorers of our Lord.

74
On Undertaking a Sea Journey

When a person embarks a boat or a ship, he should make the following supplication:

بِسْمِ اللَّـهِ مَجْرَهَا وَمُرْسَهَا اِنَّ رَبِّىْ لَغَفُوْرٌ رَّحِيْمٌ وَمَا قَدَرُوا اللَّهَ حَقَّ قَدْرِهِ وَالْاَرْضُ جَمِيْعًا قَبْضَتُهُ يَوْمَ الْقِيَمَةِ وَالسَّمٰوٰتُ مَطْوِيّٰتٌ بِيَمِيْنِهِ سُبْحَانَهُ وَتَعَالٰى عَمَّا يُشْرِكُوْنَ 0

Bismillahi majriha wa mursaha inna rabbi la ghafûrur rahim, wa ma qadarul laha haqqa qadrihi wal ardhu jamian qabdhatuhû yaumal qiyamati was samawati matwiyatum beyaminihi subhanahu wa ta ala amma yushrikun.

In the Name of Allâh its sailing and its moorning. Surely, my Lord is Forgiving, Merciful and they honour not Allâh with the honour due to Him and the whole earth will be in His grip on the Day of Resurrection and the heavens rolled up in His right hand. Glory be to Him! And highly exalted is He above what they associate (with Him).

75

While Entering a City

اَللّٰهُمَّ بَارِكْ لَنَا فِيْهَا

Allahumma barik lana fiha (to be recited thrice).

O Allâh! bless us with it

اَللّٰهُمَّ ارْزُقْنَا جَنَاهَا وَحَبِّبْنَآ اِلٰى اَهْلِهَا وَحَبِّبْ
صَالِحِیْ اَهْلِهَآ اِلَیْنَا

Allâhummar zuqna janaha wa habbibna
ila ahliha wa habbib salihî ahliha ilaina.

O Allâh! Bless us in this (township). O
Allâh! Provide us with the fruits thereof.

And cause us to be loved by the folk
thereof and cause the righteous folk
thereof to be loved by us.

76
At the Time of Landing
at a place

رَبِّ اَنْزِلْنِیْ مُنْزَلًا مُّبَارَكًا وَّاَنْتَ خَیْرُ الْمُنْزِلِیْنَ

Rabbi anzilni munzalam mubarakan wa
anta khairul munzilîn

My Lord! Cause me to land at the
landing blest and Thou art the best of
those who bring to land.

77

اَعُوْذُ بِكَلِمَاتِ اللّٰهِ التَّآمَّاتِ مِنْ شَرِّ مَا خَلَقَ

Aûzu bi kalimatillahit tâmmati min sharri ma khalaqa

I seek refuge in the perfect words of Allâh from the evil of that which He hath created.

78

At the Time of Instructing a New Convert to Islam.

اَللّٰهُمَّ اغْفِرْلِىْ وَارْحَمْنِىْ وَاهْدِنِىْ وَارْزُقْنِىْ

Allâhummaghfirli war hamni wahdini war zuqni

O Allâh! Grant me pardon, have mercy on me, guide me (to the right path) and grant me livelihood.

79

At the Time of coming back from a Journey to One's Home

تَوْبًا تَوْبًا لِّرَبِّنَا اَوْبًا لَا يُغَادِرُ عَلَيْنَا حَوْبًا

Tauban taubal li rabbina auban la yughadiru alaina hauban.

We offer too much repentance to our Lord; turn to Him (so that) no sin be left with us.

80

At the Time of Distress

حَسْبُنَا اللّٰهُ وَنِعْمَ الْوَكِيْلُ عَلَى اللّٰهِ تَوَكَّلْنَا

Hasbunal lâhu wa nimal wakîlu alal lahi tawakkalna.

Allâh is sufficient for us and He is an Excellent Guardian and we repose our trust in Allâh.

81

At the Time of Receiving a Shock

اِنَّ لِلّٰهِ وَ اِنَّاۤ اِلَيْهِ رَاجِعُوْنَ اَللّٰهُمَّ عِنْدَكَ اَحْتَسِبُ
مُصِيْبَتِىْ فَاجِرْنِىْ فِيْهَا وَاَبْدِلْنِىْ مِنْهَا خَيْرًا

Inna lillâhi wa inna ilaihi rajiûn. Allahumma indaka ahtasibu musîbati fa ajirni fîha wa abdilni minha khairan.

Surely we are Allâh's and to Him shall we return. O Allâh! I beseech Thee for the reward of my hardship. Reward me and compensate me by substituting it with goodness.

82

When Overwhelmed by the Awe of a Tyrant

اَللّٰهُمَّ اكْفِنَا هُمْ بِمَا شِئْتَ اَللّٰهُمَّ اِنِّىْ اَجْعَلُكَ فِىْ
نُحُوْرِهِمْ وَاَعُوْذُ بِكَ مِنْ شُرُوْرِهِمْ

Allâhummak-fina hum bima shi'ta allahumma inni ajaluka fi nuhûrihim wâ aûzubika min shurûrihim.

O Allâh! Let Thy sustenance, suffice us against them as Thou desirest. O Allâh! I place Thee in front of them, and I seek refuge in Thee from their mischief.

83
For Relief in Hardship

اَللَّهُمَّ لَا سَهْلَ إِلَّا مَا جَعَلْتَهُ سَهْلًا وَّأَنْتَ تَجْعَلُ الْحُزْنَ سَهْلًا إِذَا شِئْتَ.

Allahumma la sahla illa ma ja-altahu sahlan wa anta taja-lul huzna sahlan iza shi'ta.

O Allâh! There is nothing easy except what Thou so maketh and Thou maketh the difficult easy, whatsoever Thou liketh.

84

For the Fulfilment of a Need or Desire

اَللّٰهُمَّ اِنِّیْ اَسْئَلُكَ اَتَوَجَّهُ اِلَیْكَ بِنَبِیِّكَ مُحَمَّدٍ نَّبِیِّ
الرَّحْمَةِ فِیْ حَاجَتِیْ هٰذِهٖ لِتُقْضٰی لِیْ فَشَفِّعْهُ فِیَّ

Allahumma inni asaluka atawajjahu ilaika be nabi-yyika Muhammadin nabiyyir-rahmati fi hâjati hâzihî lî tuqdha lî fashaffihû fea.

O Allâh! I beseech Thee and approach Thee through Muhammad, the Prophet of mercy and be Thee to fulfil my need so that the Prophet's intercession may be completed in my favour.

85
For Forgiveness

اَللّٰهُمَّ مَغْفِرَتُكَ اَوْسَعُ مِنْ ذُنُوبِىْ وَرَحْمَتُكَ اَرْجَى عِنْدِىْ مِنْ عَمَلِىْ٥

Allâhumma maghfiratuka ausa-'u min zunûbî wa rahmatuka arjâ 'indî min 'amalî.

O Allâh! The extent of Thy forgiven-ess is far wider as compared to my sins and the extent of Thy mercy is a matter of greater hope for me than my deed.

86
At the Time of Drought

اَللّٰهُمَّ اَسْقِنَا اَللّٰهُمَّ اَغِثْنَاه٥

Allâhumma asqinâ Allâhumma aghisna.

O Allâh! Give us the drink. O Allâh! Bless us with rainfall.

87

On Seeing Clouds

اَللّٰهُمَّ اِنَّا نَعُوْذُ بِكَ مِنْ شَرِّ مَآ اُرْسِلَ بِهٖ

Allâhumma innâ na'ûzubika min sharri mâ ursila bihi.

O Allâh! We seek refuge in Thee from the evil of that which hath been sent there with.

88

At the Time of Rainfall

اَللّٰهُمَّ صَيِّبًا نَافِعًا

Allâhumma sayyiban nâfi-an.

O Allâh! Make it a profitable downpour.

89

When there is an Excessive Downpour

اَللّٰهُمَّ حَوَالَيْنَا وَلَا عَلَيْنَا اَللّٰهُمَّ عَلَى الْاٰكَامِ وَالْاٰجَامِ وَالظِّرَابِ وَالْاَوْدِيَةِ وَمَنَا بِتِ الشَّجَرِ

*Allâhumma hawalainâ wa lâ 'alainâ
Allâhumma 'alal âkâmi wal âjâmi waz-zarâbi
wal audiyati wa manabitash-shajari.*

O Allâh! Let there be downpour in our
suburbs but not on us. Let the rain fall on
hillocks in the thickets on the mountains,
rivers and on the hotbeds of plantations.

90
When one hears Thunders

اَللّٰهُمَّ لَا تَقْتُلْنَا بِغَضَبِكَ وَلَا تُهْلِكْنَا بِعَذَابِكَ وَعَافِنَا
قَبْلَ ذَالِكَ٥

*Allâhumma lâ taqtulnâ bi ghadhabika wa
lâ tuhliknâ bi 'azâbika wa 'âfina qabla zâlika.*

O Allâh! Slay us not with Thy wrath
and destroy us not with Thy punishment
but forgive us before that.

91

سُبْحَانَ الَّذِىْ يُسَبِّحُ الرَّعْدُ بِحَمْدِهِ وَالْمَلَئِكَةُ
مِنْ خِيْفَتِهِ٥

Glory, be unto He (Allâh) whose praise the thunder hymneth and the angels (hymn) out of awe of Him.

92
In Darkness and Storm

اَللّٰهُمَّ اِنَّا نَسْئَلُكَ مِنْ خَيْرِ هٰذِهِ الرِّيحِ وَخَيْرِ مَا فِيهَا

وَخَيْرِ مَآ أُمِرَتْ بِهٖ وَنَعُوْذُبِكَ مِنْ شَرِّ هٰذِهِ الرِّيحِ

وَشَرِّ مَا فِيهَا وَ شَرِّ مَآ أُمِرَتْ بِهٖ ٥

Allâhumma innâ nas'aluka min khairi hâzihir-rîhi wa khairi mâ fîhâ wa khaire mâ umirat bihî wa na'ûzubika min sharri hâzihir-rîhi wa sharri mâ fîhâ wa sharri mâ umirat behî

O Allâh! We beg to Thee the good of this wind and the good of that which is therein and the good of that which it path been hidden and we seek refuge in Thee from the evil of this wind, and the evil of that which it hath hidden.

93
On Hearing the Crowing

اَللّٰهُمَّ اِنِّى اَسْئَلُكَ مِنْ فَضْلِكَ٥

Allâhumma innî as'aluka min fazlika.

O Allah! I beg of Thee Thy bounty.

94
On Hearing a Donkey Bray or a Dog Bark

اَعُوْذُ بِاللّٰهِ مِنَ الشَّيْطٰنِ الرَّجِيْمِ٥

A'ûzubillâhi minash-shaitânir-rajîm.

I seek refuge in Allâh from Satan the outcast.

95
When there is Solar or Lunar Eclipse.

One should hymn the glory of Allâh by saying اَللّٰهُ اَكْبَرُ *Allâh-u-Akbar* (Allâh is Great), offer prayers, and give charity and alms.

96
On Sighting the New Moon

اَللّٰهُمَّ اَهِلَّهُ عَلَيْنَا بِالْيُمْنِ وَالْاِيْمَانِ وَالسَّلَامَةِ وَالْاِسْلَامِ وَالتَّوْفِيْقِ لِمَا تُحِبُّ وَتَرْضٰى رَبِّىْ وَرَبُّكَ اللّٰهُ०

Allâhumma ahillahû 'ainâ bil yumni wal îmâni was-salâmati wal islâmi wat-taufiqui limâ tuhibbu wa tarzâ rabbi wa rabbukal-lâhu.

O Allâh! Let this new moon appear unto us with good luck and prosperity, with faith, with safety and with Islam and with hope of success to do deeds which my Lord and your (moon's) Lord likes and approves.

97
On Beholding The Moon

اَعُوْذُ بِاللّٰهِ مِنْ شَرِّ هٰذَا الْغَاسِقِ

A'ûzubillâhi min sharri hâzal ghâsiqi

I seek refuge in Allâh from the evil of this darkness.

98
On Shabe Qadr

اَللّٰهُمَّ اِنَّكَ عَفُوٌّ تُحِبُّ الْعَفْوَ فَاعْفُ عَنِّیْ

Allâhumma innaka 'afuwun tuhibbul 'afwa-fâ-'afu 'anni.

O Allâh! Verily, Thou art pardoner, Thou lovest pardon so grant me forgiveness.

99
On Seeing One's Face in the Looking Glass

اَللّٰهُمَّ اَنْتَ حَسَّنْتَ خَلْقِىْ فَحَسِّنْ خُلُقِىْ

Allâhumma anta has-santa khalqî fa hassin khuluqî ۰

O Allâh! Thou made my physical constitution quite good, make my disposition good too.

100
When One is Reminded of the Other Person

اَللّٰهُمَّ صَلِّ عَلٰى مُحَمَّدٍ ذَكَرَ اللّٰهُ بِخَيْرٍ مَّنْ ذَكَرَنِىْ

Allâhumma Salli 'alâ Muhammadin zakarallâhu bi khairim man zakaranî.

O Allâh! Shower Thy blessings on Muhammad let Allah bear well in mind one who remembered me.

101
When a Muslim Seeks Another Muslim With Cheerful Countenance

أَضْحَكَ اللَّهُ سِنَّكَ

Az-hakallâhu sinnaka.

May Allâh always keep you cheerful!

102
When any Favour is done unto you

جَزَاكَ اللَّهُ خَيْرًا

Jazâkallâhu Khairan

May Allâh give you a good reward!

103
On Receiving the Debt

أَوْفَيْتَنِى أَوْ فَى اللَّهُ بِكَ

Aufaitanî aufallâhu bika.

You paid me my due; let Allâh fulfil (His promise) unto you.

104
When a Man Finds anything in Accordance with His Wishes.

اَلْحَمْدُ لِلّٰهِ الَّذِى بِنِعْمَتِهِ تَتِمُّ الصَّلِحٰتُ

Alhamdu-lil-lâhil-lazî bi ne'matihî tatimmus sâlihâtu.

All praise be to Allâh with whose benevolence the good things lead to perfection.

105
When One Finds Anything Disagreeable.

اَلْحَمْدُ لِلّٰهِ عَلٰى كُلِّ حَالٍ

Alhamdu lil lâhi 'alâ kulli hâlin.

Praise be to Allâh under all sects of conditions.

106

When Evil Thoughts
Come to Mind

اَعُوذُ بِاللّٰهِ مِنَ الشَّيْطٰنِ اٰمَنْتُ بِاللّٰهِ وَرُسُلِهٖ

A'ûzubillâhi minash-shaitâni âmantu billâhi wa rusulihî.

I take refuge with Allâh from the Satan. I repose my faith in Allâh and His apostles.

107

At the Time of Anger

اَعُوذُ بِاللّٰهِ مِنَ الشَّيْطٰنِ الرَّجِيْمِ

A'ûzubillâhi minash-shaitânir rajîm

I take refuge in Allâh from the Satan outcast.

108
For the Expiation of Sins (of the Tongue) Committed in an Assembly

سُبْحَانَ اللّٰهِ وَبِحَمْدِهٖ سُبْحَانَكَ اللّٰهُمَّ وَبِحَمْدِكَ

اَشْهَدُ اَنْ لَّا إِلٰهَ إِلَّا اَنْتَ اَسْتَغْفِرُكَ وَاَتُوْبُ اِلَيْكَ.

Subhânal-lâhi- wa bi hamdihî Subhâna-kallâ humma wa bi hamdika ash-hadu allâ ilâha illâ anta astaghfiruka wa atûbu ilaika.

Glory be to Allâh and praise unto Him. Thy Glory I extol, O Allâh! and Thy praise I hymn. I testify that there is no god save Thee. I seek Thy forgiveness and unto Thee do I turn penitent.

109
Before Entering the Market

بِسْمِ اللّٰهِ اَللّٰهُمَّ اِنِّیْ اَسْئَلُكَ خَيْرَ هٰذِهِ السُّوْقِ

وَخَيْرَ مَا فِيْهَا وَاَعُوْذُ بِكَ مِنْ شَرِّ مَا فِيْهَا اَللّٰهُمَّ اِنِّیْ

اَعُوْذُبِكَ اَنْ أُصِيْبَ فِيْهَا يَمِيْنًا فَاجِرَةً اَوْ صَفْقَةً
خَاسِرَةً.

*Bismillâhi allâhumma inni as'aluka
khaira hâzihis-sûqi wa khaira mâ fîhâ wa
'aûzubika min sharri mâ fîhâ Allâhumma
innî 'aûzubika an usîba fîhâ yamînan
fâjiratan au safaqatan khâsiratan.*

In the Name of Allâh. O Allâh! I ask of
Thee good of this market and the good of
that which is therein and I seek refuge of
its evil and the evil of that which is there
in and I seek refuge in Thee lest I should
strike a bargain therein incurring loss.

110
On Beholding a Fruit of
Season for the First Time

اَللّٰهُمَّ بَارِكْ لَنَا فِىْ ثَمَرِنَا وَبَارِكْ لَنَا فِىْ مَدِيْنَتِنَا
وَبَارِكْ لَنَا فِىْ صَاعِنَا وَبَارِكْ لَنَا فِىْ مُدِّنَا.

Allâhumma bârik lanâ fî Samarinâ wa bârik lanâ fî madînatinâ wa bârik lanâ fî sâ-'inâ wa bârik lanâ fî muddinâ.

O Allâh! Bless us in our fruits, bless us in our city, bless us in our Sa's and bless its in our mudd.

111
On Finding Anyone in Affliction

اَلْحَمْدُ لِلّٰهِ الَّذِىْ عَافَانِىْ مِمَّا ابْتَلَاكَ بِهِ وَفَضَّلَنِىْ عَلىٰ كَثِيْرٍ مِمَّنْ خَلَقَ تَفْضِيْلًا ٥

Alhamdu lil-lâhil lazî 'âfânî mimmab talaka bihî wa faz-zalanî 'alâ kasîrim mimman khalaqa tafzîla

Praise be to Allâh Who saved me from that therewith He hath afflicted thee and made me to excel with a marked excellence most of those whom He created.

112
When Anything is Lost or Somebody Absconds.

اَللّٰهُمَّ رَآدَّ الضَّالَّةِ وَهَادِىَ الضَّلَالَةِ اَنْتَ تَهْدِىْ

مِنَ الضَّلَالَةِ اُرْدُدْ عَلَـىَّ ضَآلَّتِـىْ بِقُدْرَتِكَ

وَسُلْطَانِكَ فَاِنَّهَا مِنْ عَطَآئِكَ وَفَضْلِكَ ٥

Allâhumma râddaz-zâllati wa hâdiyaz-zalâlati anta tahdî minaz-zalâlati urdud allayya zâl-latî bi-qudratika wa sultânika fa inna hâ min 'atâ'ika wa fazlika.

O Allâh! Thou art the restorer of the thing, lost and Thou art the Guide to one who is in Error. Thou guideth (to the path of righteousness) one who is led astray. Restore me with Thy power and might my lost thing. For verily that was out of Thy gift and bounty.

113
When One Apprehends
on Omen

اَللَّهُمَّ لَا يَأْتِى بِالْحَسَنَاتِ اِلَّا اَنْتَ وَلَا يَذْهَبُ

بِالسَّيِّآتِ اِلَّا اَنْتَ وَلَا حَوْلَ وَلَا قُوَّةَ اِلَّا بِكَ.

*Allâhumma lâyâtî bil hasanâti illâ anta
walâ yazhabu bis-sayyiâti illâ anta wa lâ
haula walâ quwwata illâ bika.*

O Allâh! None brings good but Thee
alone and non takes away evil but Thee
alone. There is no strength nor power
save with Thee.

114
To Ward Off an Evil Eye

بِسْمِ اللهِ اَللَّهُمَّ اذْهِبْ حَرَّهَا وَبَرْدَهَا وَوَصَبَهَا.

*Bismillâhi Allâhum-mazhib harrahâ wa
bardahâ wasabahâ.*

In the name of Allâh. O Allâh! Take away its heat and cold and its pain.

115
Exorcising an Evil Spirit.

أَذْهِبِ الْبَاسَ رَبَّ النَّاسِ وَاشْفِ اَنْتَ الشَّافِيْ لَا

شَافِيَ اِلَّا اَنْتَ.

Azhibil bâsa rabban-nâsi-wâshfi antash-shâfi lâ shâ-fiya illâ anta.

O the Nourisher and Sustainer of mankind! Remove affliction, cure (him); thou art the Curer, there is no curer but Thee.

116
When Fire Breaks Out

On such occasions one should repeat.

Allâhu-Akbar اَللّٰهُ اَكْبَرُ (Allâh is Great) again and again.

117
When One Feels Pain in Kidney Due to Stone

رَبُّنَا اللّٰهُ الَّذِى فِى السَّمَآءِ تَقَدَّسَ اسْمُكَ أَمْرُكَ فِى
السَّمَآءِ وَالْأَرْضِ كَمَا رَحْمَتُكَ فِى السَّمَآءِ فَاجْعَلْ
رَحْمَتَكَ فِى الْأَرْضِ وَاغْفِرْلَنَا حُوْبَنَا وَخَطَايَانَا
أَنْتَ رَبُّ الطَّيِّبِيْنَ فَأَنْزِلْ شِفَآءً مِّنْ شِفَائِكَ وَرَحْمَةً
مِّنْ رَّحْمَتِكَ عَلىٰ هٰذَا الْوَجْعِ

Rabbu-nallâhul lazî fis-smâ-'i taqaddasa ismuka amruka fis-sama-'i wal arzi kamâ rahmatuka fis-samâ-'i faj'al rahmataka fil arzi waghfirlanâ hûbanâ wa khatayânâ anta rabbut tayyibîna fa anzil shifâ'am min shifâ-ika wa rahmatam mir-rahmatika 'alâ hâzal waj-'i.

Our Lord is Allâh, He Who is in Heaven. Hallowed be Thy name. Thine is the command in the Heaven and upon the earth. Even as Thy mercy prevail in the Heavens so let Thy mercy prevail upon the earth. Forgive our sins and failings Thou art the Lord of the Well-disposed. Send down cure from Thy cure and mercy from Thy mercy for this ailment.

118
For Sores and Swellings

Apply some saliva on the index finger and then besmear it with dust and roll it over the sore and the swelling and supplicate in the following words:

بِسْمِ اللّٰهِ تُرْبَةُ اَرْضِنَا بِرِيْقَةِ بَعْضِنَا لِيُشْفٰى

سَقِيْمُنَا بِاذْنِ رَبِّنَا

Bismillâhi turbatu arzinâ bi rîqati bazinâ li yushfâ saqîmunâ bi izni rabbinâ.

In the name of Allâh. This is the dust of our earth, With saliva of one amongst

us, so that our ailment maybe cured,
With the permission of Allah.

119
When the Feet are Benumbed

صَلَّى اللّٰهُ عَلَى مُحَمَّدٍ صَلَّى اللّٰهُ عَلَيْهِ وَاٰلِهٖ وَسَلَّمَ

*Sallal-lâhu 'alâ muhammadin sallal-lâhu
'alaihi wa âlihî wa sallam.*

Let there be blessing of Allâh upon
Muhammad, blessings of Allâh upon
him and his family and peace too.

120
For Safeguarding Ourself
Against all Types of Diseases

بِسْمِ اللّٰهِ اَعُوْذُ بِاللّٰهِ وَقُدْرَتِهٖ مِنْ شَرِّ مَآ اَجِدُ
وَاُحَاذِرُ

*Bismillâhi 'aûzubillâhi wa qudratihî min
sharrimâ ajidu wa-uhâziru.*

In the name of Allah. I seek refuge with Allah and with His power from every evil that I may find or the fear of which ever haunts me. (To be repeated seven times).

121
When Eyes are Swollen

اَللّٰهُمَّ مَتِّعْنِیْ بِبَصَرِیْ وَاجْعَلْهُ الْوَارِثَ مِنِّیْ وَأَرِنِیْ

فِی الْعَدُوِّ ثَارِیْ وَانْصُرْنِیْ عَلٰی مَنْ ظَلَمَنِیْ.

Allâhumma matti'nî bi basarî waj 'al hul wârisa minnî wa arinî fil 'adduwwi sârî wansurnî 'alâ manzalamanî.

O Allâh! Gratify me with my eyesight and make it survive after me, and show me my striving against the enemy; and grant me victory over him, who perpetrates oppression on me.

122
When a Man Suffers From Fever

بِسْمِ اللَّهِ الْكَبِيرِ اَعُوذُ بِاللَّهِ الْعَظِيمِ مِنْ شَرِّ كُلِّ

عِرْقٍ نَعَّارٍ وَّمِنْ شَرِّ حَرِّ النَّارِ٥

Bismillâhil kabîri 'aûzubillâhil 'azîmi min sharri kulli irqin n'ârinw-wa min sharri harrin nâri.

In the name of Allâh, the Great. I take refuge with Allâh, The Magnificent, from the evil of every spurting vein and from the evil of the heat of fire.

123
On Visiting the Sick

لَا بَأْسَ طَهُورٌ اِنْ شَآءَ اللهُ لَا بَأْسَ طَهُورٌ اِنْ شَآءَ

اللهُ اَللَّهُمَّ اشْفِهِ اَللَّهُمَّ عَافِهِ٥

Lâ bâ'sa tahûrun inshâ allâhu lâ bâ'sa tahûrun inshâ allâhu Allâhummash-fihî Allâhumma 'âfihî.

Mind it not! It is a purger. If Allah so wills, mind it not! It is a purger. If Allah so wills. O Allah! Cure him and recuperate him.

124
At the time of Death

لَا اِلٰهَ اِلَّا اللّٰهُ مُحَمَّدٌ رَّسُوْلُ اللّٰهِ۰

La ilâha illal-lâhu Muhammadur rasûlullâh.

There is no god save Allâh, And Muhammad is Messenger of Allâh.

125
At the Time of Condolence

اِنَّ لِلّٰهِ مَآ اَخَذَ وَلِلّٰهِ مَآ اَعْطٰى وَكُلٌّ عِنْدَهُ بِاَجَلٍ
مُّسَمًّى فَلْتَصْبِرُوْا وَلْتَحْتَسِبْ

Innalillâhi mâ akhaza wa lillâhi mâ a'atu wa kullun 'indahû bi ajalim musamman fal tasbiru wal tahtasib

Verily everything belongs to Allah that He hath taken away and belongs to Allah that He hath given. Allah is with him for an appointed time; forbear and expect reward.

126
When the Dead Body is Lowered into the Grave

بِسْمِ اللّٰهِ وَعَلٰى مِلَّةِ رَسُوْلِ اللّٰهِ

Bismillâhi wa 'alâ millati rasûlil-lâh.

In the name of Allâh and in according with the ritual of the Messenger of Allâh.

127
On Visiting the Graveyard

اَلسَّلَامُ عَلَيْكُمْ يَاۤاَهْلَ الْقُبُوْرِ يَغْفِرُ اللّٰهُ لَنَا وَلَكُمْ اَنْتُمْ سَلَفُنَا وَ نَحْنُ بِالْاَثَرِ

Assalâmu 'alaikum yâ ahlal

yaghfirul-lâhu walakum antum salafunâ wa nahnu bil asari.

Peace be upon you. O ye dwellers of these graves! May Allâh forgive us and you! You are our forerunners and we are at your heels.

128
For the Fulfilment of a Need or Desire

It is narrated on the authority of 'Abdulla bin Abi' Aufa (may Allâh be pleased with him!) that Holy Prophet (Sal-am) said: whosoever has a need that can be fulfilled by God, let him make ablution and let him make it well. Then he should offer two Rak'ats of prayer, glorify Allah, and invoke blessings on the Apostle of Allâh, thereafter supplicate in the following words:

لَا إِلٰهَ إِلَّا اللّٰهُ الْحَلِيْمُ الْكَرِيْمُ سُبْحَانَ اللّٰهِ رَبِّ

الْعَرْشِ الْعَظِيْمِ ٥ وَالْحَمْدُ لِلّٰهِ رَبِّ الْعٰلَمِيْنَ ٥

اَسْئَلُكَ مُوْجِبَاتِ رَحْمَتِكَ وَعَزَائِمَ مَغْفِرَتِكَ

وَالْغَنِيْمَةَ مِنْ كُلِّ بِرٍّ وَّالسَّلَامَةَ مِنْ كُلِّ اِثْمٍ لَّا تَدَعْ

لِىْ ذَنْبًا اِلَّا غَفَرْتَهٗ وَلَا هَمًّا اِلَّا فَرَّجْتَهٗ وَلَا حَاجَةً

هِىَ لَكَ رِضًا اِلَّا قَضَيْتَهَا يَآ اَرْحَمَ الرَّاحِمِيْنَ ٥

Lâ ilâha illal-lâhul halîmul karîmu
subhânallâhi rabbil 'arshil 'azîm, wal
hamdulillâhi rabbil 'âlamîn. As'aluka mujî
bâti rahmatika wa 'azâ-'ima maghfiratika
wal ghanîmata min kulli birrinw was-
salâmata min kulli ismin lâ tada'a lî zamban
illâ ghafartahû walâ hamman illâ farrajtahû
walâ hâjatan hiya laka rizan illâ qazaitahâ yâ
arhamarrâhimîn.

There is no god save Allâh, The
Clement, The Bountiful. Glory be to
Allah, Lord of The Magnificent Throne.
Praise be to Allâh, Lord of the worlds! I

beg of Thee the causes entailing Thy mercy and the purposes of (securing) Thy pardon, gains from every righteousness.

129
For Relief From Indebtedness

اَللّٰهُمَّ اكْفِنِىْ بِحَلَالِكَ عَنْ حَرَامِكَ وَاَغْنِىْ بِفَضْلِكَ عَنْ مَّنْ سِوَاكَ.

Allâhummakfinî be halâlika 'an harâmika wa aghnî bi fazlika amman siwâka.

O Allâh! let Thy sublimity suffice me against things unlawful unto Thee. Make me, by Thy grace, dependant on none save Thyself.

130
For the Relief of Pain

وَبِالْحَقِّ اَنْزَلْنٰهُ وَبِالْحَقِّ نَزَلَ وَمَآ اَرْسَلْنٰكَ اِلَّا
مُبَشِّرًا وَّنَذِيْرًاo

Wa bilhaqqi anzalnâhu wa bil haqqi nazala wamâ arsalnâka illâ mubash-shiranw wa nazîra.

And with truth have we revealed it. And with truth did it come, and we have not sent thee, but as a giver of glad tidings and as a warner.

131
For Improvement of Eyesight

Daily after the five Farz Prayers, recite eleven times the words:

ya nûru يَا نُوْر (O Light) and place the end of your fingers on your eyes.

132
For Stammering

Recite the following prayer for 21 times after the morning prayer:

رَبِّ اشْرَحْ لِى صَدْرِى ٥ وَيَسِّرْلِى أَمْرِى ٥ وَاحْلُلْ
عُقْدَةً مِّنْ لِّسَانِى ٥ يَفْقَهُوا قَوْلِى ٥

Rabbishrah lî sadrî wa yassir lî amri wahlul 'uqdatam millisâni yaf qahû qaulî.

O My Lord! Expand me my breast. Ease my task for me and remove the impediment from my speech, so that they may understand what I say.

133
For the Relief of Stomach-Ache

Recite three times the following words from Holy Qur'an over water and make the sufferer drink it:

لَا فِيْهَا غَوْلٌ وَّلَا هُمْ عَنْهَا يُنْزِفُوْنَ ٥

La feeha ghaulun walahum anha yunzafoon.

It deprives not of reason nor are they exhausted therewith.

134
When the Epidemics Like Cholera and Plague Break Out

During these calamities before eating anything recite the following Surah three times.

اِنَّآ اَنْزَلْنٰهُ فِىْ لَيْلَةِ الْقَدْرِ وَمَآ اَدْرٰكَ مَالَيْلَةُ الْقَدْرِ لَيْلَةُالْقَدْرِ، خَيْرٌمِّنْ اَلْفِ شَهْرٍ، تَنَزَّلُ الْمَلٰئِكَةُ وَالرُّوْحُ فِيْهَا بِاِذْنِ رَبِّهِمْ مِّنْ كُلِّ اَمْرٍ سَلٰمٌ، هِىَ حَتّٰى مَطْلَعِ الْفَجْرِ

Innâ anzalnâhu fî lailatil qadri. wamâ adrâka ma lailatul qadr. lailatul qadri khairum-min alfi shahr, tanaz-zalul malâ'ikatu; warrûhu fîhâ bi izni rabbihim

*min kulli 'amrin, salâmun-hiya hatta matla-
'ilfajr.*

In the name of Allâh, The Beneficent,
The Merciful. Surely we have revealed it
on the night of Majesty. And what will
make thee comprehend. What the night
of Majesty is? The Night of Majesty is
better than a thousand months. The
angels and the spirit descend in it by the
permission of their Lord. For every
affair: peace it is till the rising of morn.

If a person falls a victim to these
epidemics the above verses may be recited over any eatables and the patient
asked to eat them.

135
For Relief From Fever

قُلْنَا يَا نَارُكُوْنِيْ بَرْدًا وَّ سَلَمًا عَلَى إِبْرَاهِيْمَ

*Qulnâ yâ nâru kûnî bardanw wa salâman
'alâ Ibrahima*

We said! O fire! Be coolness and peace for Abraham.

136

In case a person runs temperature with coldness, the following words of Qur'an should be recited:

بِسْمِ اللّٰهِ مَجْرِهَا وَمُرْسٰهَا اِنَّ رَبِّى لَغَفُوْرٌ رَّحِيْمٌ

Bismillâhi majrîhâ wa mursâhâ inna rabbî la ghafûrur-rahîm.

In the name of Allâh. Be its sailing and its mooring. Verily my Lord is indeed Forgiving and Merciful.

137
When Bitten by Snake, Scorpion, or Wasp

Touch the bitten place slightly after dipping a finger in the solution of salt and recite this verse seven times:

بِسْمِ اللهِ الرَّحْمٰنِ الرَّحِيمِ ٥ قُلْ يَآأَيُّهَا الْكَٰفِرُوْنَ ٥
لَآ أَعْبُدُ مَا تَعْبُدُوْنَ ٥ وَلَآ أَنْتُمْ عَٰبِدُوْنَ مَآ أَعْبُدُ ٥ وَلَآ
أَنَا عَابِدٌ مَّا عَبَدْتُّمْ ٥ وَلَآ أَنْتُمْ عَٰبِدُوْنَ مَآ أَعْبُدُ ٥
لَكُمْ دِيْنُكُمْ وَلِىَ دِيْنِ ٥

*Bismillâhir-rahmânir-rahîm, qul yâ
ayyuhal kâfirûna lâ 'âbudu mâ ta'abudûna
walâ antum 'âbidûna mâ 'abud, walâ anâ
'âbidum mâ abat tum walâ antum 'âbidûna
mâ 'abud, lakum dînukum waliya dîn.*

In the name of Allâh, The Beneficent,
The Merciful. Say: O disbelievers! I
worship not that which ye worship; nor
do ye worship Him, whom I worship,
nor shall I worship that which, ye have
been wont to worship, no will ye
worship Him whom I worship. To you
be your way and to me mine.

138
When Bitten by a Mad Dog

Write these words of the Qur'an on a biscuit and offer it to the man who has been bitten by a mad dog and ask him to eat it.

اِنَّهُمْ يَكِيدُوْنَ كَيْدًا وَّاَكِيدُ كَيْدًا ٥ فَمَهِّلِ الْكٰفِرِيْنَ

اَمْهِلْهُمْ رُوَيْدًا٥

Innahum yakîdûna kaidanw wa akîdu kaidâ, famah-hilil kâfirîna amhil-hum ruwaida.

As for them, they are but plotting a scheme and I am planning a shcheme; so grant the disbelievers, a respite-let them alone for a while.

139
For Relief of Every Kind of Aliment

Write Surah Fatiha and these verses on a china plate and then solve them in water and ask the patient to drink it.

وَيَشْفِ صُدُورَ قَوْمٍ مُّؤْمِنِينَ وَإِذَا مَرِضْتُ فَهُوَ
يَشْفِينِ ٥ وَشِفَاءٌ لِّمَا فِى الصُّدُورِ وَهُدًى وَّرَحْمَةٌ
لِّلْمُؤْمِنِينَ ٥ وَنُنَزِّلُ مِنَ الْقُرْآنِ مَا هُوَ شِفَاءٌ
وَّرَحْمَةٌ لِّلْمُؤْمِنِينَ ٥ وَلَا يَزِيدُ الظَّالِمِينَ إِلَّا
خَسَارًا ٥ قُلْ هُوَ لِلَّذِينَ آمَنُوا هُدًى وَّشِفَاءٌ ٥

Wa yashfi sudûra qaumim mu'minîn wa izâ marizto fahuwa yashfîna. Wa shifâ-ul limâ fis-sudûri wa hudanw wa rahmatul-lil mu'minîn. wa nunaz-zilu minal qur'âni mâ huwa shifâ-'un wa rahmatul- lil muminîn walâ yazîduz-zâlimîna illâ khasâra. qul huwa lil-lazîna âmanu hudanw wa shifâ-un.

Relieve the hearts of a believing people and when I am sick, He heals me; and a healing for what is in the breasts; and a guidance and a mercy to the believers. And We reveal of the Qur'an that which is a healing and a mercy to the believers and it adds only to the predition of wrong-doers. Say it is to those who believe a guidance and healing.

140
When One is Influenced by an Evil Eye

Recite the following Surahs three times:

قُلْ اَعُوْذُ بِرَبِّ الْفَلَقِ ٥ مِنْ شَرِّ مَا خَلَقَ ٥ وَمِنْ
شَرِّ غَاسِقٍ اِذَا وَقَبَ ٥ وَمِنْ شَرِّ النَّفّٰثٰتِ فِى
الْعُقَدِ ٥ وَمِنْ شَرِّ حَاسِدٍ اِذَا حَسَدَ ٥ قُلْ اَعُوْذُ
بِرَبِّ النَّاسِ ٥ مَلِكِ النَّاسِ ٥ اِلٰهِ النَّاسِ ٥ مِنْ شَرِّ
الْوَسْوَاسِ الْخَنَّاسِ ٥ الَّذِىْ يُوَسْوِسُ فِى صُدُوْرِ
النَّاسِ مِنَ الْجِنَّةِ وَالنَّاسِ ٥

Qul 'aûzu bi rabbil falaqi, min sharri mâ-khlalaqa wa min sharri ghâsiqin izâ waqab wa min sharrin naffâsâti fil 'uqadi, wa min sharri hâsidin izâ hasad.

Qul 'aûzu bi rabbin-nasi, malikin-nâsi, ilâhin-nâsi, min sharril was wa-sil, khannâsillazî yuwas-wisu fî sudûrin-nâsi, minal jinnati wan-nâs.

Say: I seek refuge in the Lord of the dawn from the evil of that which He hath created; and from the evil of intense darkness as it comes; and from the evil of those who cast (evil suggestions) in firm resolutions; and from the evil of the envies.

Say: I seek refuge with the Lord and Cherisher of mankind — the King of mankind, the God of mankind from the mischief of the whispering of the slinking (devil), who whispers into the hearts of men, from among the Jinn and the men.

141
When One is Influenced
by an Evil Spirit

Recite the following verses in the ear of the patient. Recite them over water too and offer him as a drink.

اَفَحَسِبْتُمْ اَنَّمَا خَلَقْنٰكُمْ عَبَثًا وَّاَنَّكُمْ اِلَيْنَا لَا تُرْجَعُوْنَ ٥ فَتَعٰلَى اللّٰهُ الْمَلِكُ الْحَقُّ لَا اِلٰهَ اِلَّا هُوَ رَبُّ الْعَرْشِ الْكَرِيْمِ ٥ وَمَنْ يَّدْعُ مَعَ اللّٰهِ اِلٰهًا اٰخَرَ لَا بُرْهَانَ لَهُ بِهٖ فَاِنَّمَا حِسَابُهُ عِنْدَ رَبِّهٖ اِنَّهُ لَا يُفْلِحُ الْكٰفِرُوْنَ ٥ وَقُلْ رَّبِّ اغْفِرْ وَارْحَمْ وَاَنْتَ خَيْرُ الرّٰحِمِيْنَ ٥

Afa hasibtum annamâ khalaqnâkum 'abasanw wa annakum ilainâ lâ turja-'ûn fata'âlallâhul malikul haqqu lâ ilâha illâ huwa rabbul 'arshil karîm. Wa man yad'û ma-'allâhi ilâhan âkhara lâ burhâna lahû bi-hee fa

Innamâ hisâbuhû 'inda rabbihî innahû lâ yuflahul kâfirûn, Wa-qul rabigh-fir warham wa anta khairur râhimîn.

Do you think that We have created you in vain and that you will not be turned to Us? So exalted be Allâh. The True King'. No god is there but He, the Lord of the Throne of Grace, and whoever invokes, besides Allah, another god; he has no proof of this. His reckoning is only with his Lord. Surely the disbelievers will not be successful and say; My Lord! Forgive those who show mercy and Thou art the Best of those who show the mercy.

THE SURAH

Was-sama-i Wat-târiqi is also efficacious for relieving a man from the influence of evil spirits. It must be recited 7 times in the ear and should be recited 7 times in the ear and should be followed by Azân in the right ear and Takbir in the left.

Glory be to Allâh; my Lord, Blessing be upon Muhammad, the greatest benefactor of mankind. Let Allâh Bless him with His choicest blessings.

OUR MOST POPULAR POCKET SIZE TITLES

Size   :   20x30/32
Price Rs. :

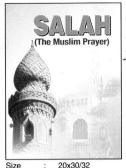

Size   :   20x30/32
Price Rs. :

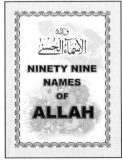

Size   :   25x36/64
Price Rs. :

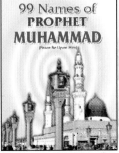

Size   :   23x36/32
Price Rs. :